Standing On Your Knees

A Faith Worth Having

Susan Rosecrans

WESTBOW
PRESS®
A DIVISION OF THOMAS NELSON
& ZONDERVAN

All Scripture quotations in this publications are from The Message. Copyright © by Eugene H. Peterson 1993, 1994, 1995, 1996, 2000, 2001, 2002. Used by permission of NavPress Publishing Group.

WestBow Press books may be ordered through booksellers or by contacting:

WestBow Press
A Division of Thomas Nelson & Zondervan
1663 Liberty Drive
Bloomington, IN 47403
www.westbowpress.com
1 (866) 928-1240

ISBN: 978-1-5127-2506-3 (sc)
ISBN: 978-1-5127-2507-0 (e)

Library of Congress Control Number: 2015921223

Print information available on the last page.

WestBow Press rev. date: 01/19/2016

Contents

To Mom

I'll see you when I get home…

Thank You

Thank you. Two of my favorite words to say, and then comes my worry "I don't want to leave anyone out!"

So here goes my attempt to thank all the people who made this book possible. I have to start with the drama team at Grace Church in Noblesville, Indiana. The thoughts that became this book were shared during our Wednesday night meetings.

To the Grace Drama team, I love each one of you. I have experienced laughter, love and beauty with you all, and most importantly, I have seen God at work in and through each one of you. I am hoping and praying you hear the beautiful music God created through this broken instrument.

To my troupe a big thank-you! You all know how much I love you! So thank you, thank you Drama Peeps for making this book a reality.

I have to give another shout out to the rest of my family at Grace church. So many of you have loved me and poured into to my heart. I want to say a special thanks to Jeff Unruh, Alison Cook, and my friend, passionate follower of Jesus, wonderfully unique, fearless leader Amy Christie. Your leadership and friendship means the world to me. You all loved me at a time my heart was so broken nothing made sense. Thank you!

I have to thank Rosalyn Carlson, Molly Mohr, Amy Kross. They read the crummy first draft. Thank you for your feedback. And thank you Nikki Lynch for going above and beyond. You helped shape the final draft.

I want to give a huge hug and a special big thanks to Nancy Hettlinger my editor and encourager! You know how much I respect and love you. This book wouldn't have made to print without you, friend. Thank you, Thank you, Thank you!

I want to thank my family and friends from the Goddard School Carmel, Indiana. I have seen such beauty in your families what a joy to watch and learn about God's love through you all.

There is a group of woman I have done life with for the past 30 years….ugh! Has it really been that long? I have to say thank you. You all taught me so much about laughing and weeping, authentic faith and persistently following Him. So thank you Laura McCollum, Roxie Crawford, Mary Beth Oblinger Lundgren, Diane Eley, my very special pal Debbie Richardson and her wonderful family and to our dear sweet friend who waits for us on the other side Jama Hottenstein, thank you all so much.

To my family, we have all been through so much. We miss our sweet Nicholas every day. We celebrate Jeremiah's return and wait with amazement as our Grace grows up. I am forever thankful for my Noah, my kindred spirit. Thank you, Noah, you saved our grieving broken family. We are all just a rescue story waiting to happen. Thank you all for loving me! Know how much I love you all.

To my Shepherd, my Redeemer, my Rescuer, my Light, my Comfort, my Sustainer, my Savior from whom all things come, I pray each day I will live faithfully and trust fully. How do I thank the one who hung the moon and the stars? With every breath I take, I whisper thank you to my amazing, evergreen-forever-more, exquisite God.

All my love to my One and Only, my Sweet Savior, my forever and my always at last

Thank you.

Warning

I know, I know most books begin with an elegant introduction. This is not that book. This book begins with a warning. The title which I fell in love with when the words tumbled into place sounds **serious** implying the book will be a heavy read on a very deep topic, faith. If you are looking for the depth of Charles Spurgeon, the challenge of Dietrich Bonhoeffer or the wisdom Dallas Willard, I suggest you read one of their amazing books. For those of you who have no idea who these guys are don't fret. I didn't know of them until a few years ago. Yes, this book is about faith, A Faith Worth Having, but it is not designed to be a complex, theory driven, intellectual ride. Nope, the cobbling of these ideas are simply one person's take on the journey of faith. Pull up a chair. Grab a cup of tea, a mug of coffee or tall frappe-delicious-ccino and let's talk.

This book came out of journeying, praying, journaling and then finally sharing my ideas with my dear friends at a Wednesday night Drama Team meeting held at Grace Church in Noblesville, Indiana. This book comes from eyes and ears that look and listen for the simple. Then, I love painting a vivid picture of what I have seen and heard. After each chapter, there is a picturesque meditation, a collection of spiritual portraits or a scenic prayer. These are to be used however you see fit. They can be a treat or a dessert after finishing each chapter. They are each written with the purpose of letting the words wash over you. Let the images cascade through your mind. Hopefully, they will encourage you and lift you up.

Finally the most basic question stands in the center of the room waiting to be answered. Why write **this** book? Many of us feel stuck unable to simply grow our faith. We struggle to develop that intangible quality that our eternal impact rests upon. I wrote this book because I have struggled to move toward a deeper faith, A Faith Worth Having. A Bible verse that has stuck with me is Mark 9:24 [24] "No sooner were the words out of his mouth than the father cried, 'Then I believe. Help me with my doubts!'[24] Immediately the boy's father exclaimed, 'I do believe; help me overcome my unbelief!" Please God, help me overcome my doubts and my unbelief has been my desperate plea.

My faith has often been shoved aside. I complain and become very frustrated at my circumstances. I struggle to respond well to others, even others I love deeply. O God, help me overcome my lack of faith. I am not an expert in faith triumphs. No, I fail more often than I succeed, but I am all in. I do desire my beliefs, my words and my actions mean something. I want to walk the talk. I want to make a difference. This book is one woman's attempt to make sense of her faith journey.

Whether you are unfamiliar with Christianity, new to the Christian faith or you are all in, it is my desire that this book will encourage you and challenge you. If you find a way to be more engaged in your new found faith, then I am exceedingly excited for you. If you find one new helpful way of living out your well-worn faith, then I have succeeded beyond measure. If you are just entering the inside out, upside down kingdom of God and after reading this book desire to learn more, then I am the one celebrating in the bleachers. And, I am the one praying your journey continues, because I am on the lookout for your forever impact.

One final warning, spending time with this material will change you.
Grab your favorite drink, sit back and let's talk about faith, A Faith Worth Having.

CHAPTER 1

Her Faith Worth Having

More than once she was seen kneeling by her bed praying-this woman of faith. Her circumstances were difficult to say the least. She and her husband of over twenty years had lost everything they owned. Their land in Colorado gone, a ten year old family business gone and their house was gone. Her husband had made poor business decisions and in an attempt to keep his business afloat he had risked everything even their home. Love had roamed the halls of this three bedroom ranch as she raised her children. This warm memory-filled home was where she planned to grow old with her husband, read books to her grandchildren and gather for each family celebration. But now defeated, depressed and broken, her husband could not find his way out. He seemed resigned to complete failure. He sat in his favorite chair. He sat doing nothing. He had absolutely given up.

She had been underemployed all her life. A cafeteria worker, a clerk in the toy department and now as a receptionist she worked so hard yet brought home very little. After years of terrible financial stress and insecurity, suddenly she was the only bread winner. It had been a brutal five years. Never bitterness, crying out yes, sadness, of course, even frustration at the tough road they were now traveling, but never ever bitterness. Why? She simply stood on her knees living out her granite strong faith.

She had what I call A Faith Worth Having. She had the ability to be her best when life was at its worst. In the midst of extremely hard life circumstances, she was living her best possible life. She could be seen calmly kneeling in reverence to her loving God. She would regularly pour out her heart to her One and Only, the One who truly mattered.

Someone looking from the outside might have questioned, "Where is this God she loves so deeply?" It would have been easy to say she had been betrayed, or the very least forgotten, left to her own devices to fend for herself during these truly lean, difficult times. She just stood firm in her faith believing her God was near. She knelt calmly, serenely trusting during the worst of times. She trusted her precious Savior to take care of her and in a daring leap of faith trusted God with those closest to her heart, those she loved so deeply, those she would live and die for, her family. Who has a faith like that? Who doesn't want a faith like that? Think of someone you know who has endured heartache with a strong, deep, sweet, real, never giving up on God, honest about the pain and the hurt faith. This is someone battered by life's worst standing on their knees holding onto The Rock that never moves. That's what I call *A Faith Worth Having.*

Faith, understanding and articulating real life-altering faith, seems as difficult as catching water with your fingers. We see water's power in oceans waves. We flinch when water is too hot. We only touch frozen water for a few seconds. We know we all need eight glasses of water a day to stay healthy. Water is huge part of our lives, yet the easiest way to describe it is when it is moving. Authentic faith is very similar. There is gritty faith that pulls people through the worst of circumstances. There is remarkable, astounding faith that sustains people for decades. There is quiet faith that endures and pushes forward never faltering. There is daring faith that leaps into the unknown, unafraid of the consequences or cost. Who wouldn't want gritty, remarkable, astounding, quiet, daring, leaping faith?

Does everyone who is a Christian have A Faith Worth Having? Have you witnessed those whose faith did not feel authentic? Their words and their actions did not match. They did not live out God's inside out, upside down kingdom. They say the right things, but their small faith was lived out in their self-created spotlight. As you listened and looked on, something didn't ring true. All kinds of faith cross our paths daily. There is a "faith" lived out where every loved one is healthy, happy, and home by 11 pm. They worship weekly, care about the less-thans and give a portion of their wealth away believing God has blessed them with wealth as a kind of spiritual seal of approval. If problems do come, they attempt to buy the answers. If that doesn't work, they pave over the hurt and heartache attempting to rewrite history while creating their new version of a happy, healthy future. Come to think about it they never really needed faith.

Some live by a faith combo platter called Jesus and_____ . Jesus and whatever makes them successful are the pillars of their faith. Their faith-life is Jesus and their happy, healthy family. Their faith-purpose is Jesus and their helpful ministry. Their faith-safe-haven is Jesus and financial security. They live a divided life. An incredibly cynical view would be to say they are simply covering all the bases, feathering every nest, not willing to risk, trust, surrender or release. They live out a half-hearted, never far from themselves untested, small faith.

Others live an *us-versus-them* Christian faith. They live a faith that only interacts with other believers. They never wade into the messiness of someone else's life. Throughout the decades, they trust in their own efforts to protect. They trust in the barriers they have built preventing any darkness from entering their secure world. They have worked hard to build each wall. They have spent everything to create their fortress. Using a spiritual blockade, they become gatekeepers only letting in what they deem is safe. Unfortunately, they have built gauzy fences, delicate walls and paper thin barricades. They exist in a faux fantasy fortress. They have the answers if only *others* would listen. They know the way if only *others* would follow. They firmly believe, "If *others* would look like us, talk like us, sing like us and worship like us, then *they* too could be blessed like us!"

We understand resting on an untested faith or an add-on faith or a blockade faith isn't a Faith Worth Having, right? Can we honestly see us-versus-*others* making an impact in His inside out, upside down kingdom? Others? Who is our Others? If you and I live by the truth "there but by God's grace go I" then seriously, we all are just one decision from making a huge mistake tumbling into *others'* status. We want to make sense of all the suffering. Believing we can have complete control, we think we are the ones determining whether the bad things can happen to us. We sideline our faith. We spend our energies trying to make everything wonderful or at the very least good. We live in perpetual motion by trying to make everyone happy. We believe we can create a holy bubble or some kind of spiritual buffer to will keep the tragic stuff away from us and away from our loved ones. Most of us hope and pray, if tragedy does strike, we will hold up well. Honestly, we would do anything to keep brokenness far, far from our loves, our little loves, our big loves, our new loves, our lifetime loves and our forever loves.

Many of us struggle to balance our faith life with our everyday life. We assume they are separate. We create a combo platter faith. We never edge out of our fortified us-versus-others world. Puny, scrawny, frail, tired, pathetic faith, who wants that kind of faith? Most of us are limping along trying to live out our faith in triumphant, but we cannot. We are stumbling, struggling and overwhelmed. When we fail, we determine to simply work harder at our faith and by working harder we will be guaranteed health and happiness for ourselves and our dear ones.

When the unbelievable happens and when the hard times do hit, a little stunned almost in disbelief, we ask "Why do bad things happen to good people? Why did this happen to me and to mine?" We ask as if we believe we should be given a pass, a warning and a way out when it comes to hardships. Life is supposed to be challenging but not bone-crushing hard! When it gets dark, thick, heavy and sadness feels like deep waters, we may become angry with God for allowing this unrelenting pain. Our feelings are not out of line, but sometimes our responses are. We pull in, blame out and complain. Rejecting God's right to take us through whatever He chooses can cause us to travel away from Him and away from His peace. Jesus, author of A Faith Worth Having, told us to give way to our broken heart, to cry out and to weep. It's okay to moan, lament, whimper, whine and even shriek out in pain. After our authentic cries are over, once our soul has unloaded, then we are called to free fall into His ever-present arms. We often wrestle and even repel against crying out in pain. Tragedy and heartache can move us closer to freedom and joy, not further away. Fight, win, heal the broken are the only battle cries we think we are to follow. No one wants their motivational poster to read-wail, weep, freak out then free fall.

What keeps you and I from a gritty, remarkable, astounding, quiet, daring, leap into the unknown faith? Maybe our untested, combo platter, us-versus-others, blinded by our excuses, false sense of security faith-life may be a good place to start. Or the focusing on our obsession with control might be another good starting point. Until we can see what is locking us up, keeping us from being our best when life is at its worst, we will stay stuck with a puny, scrawny, frail, tired, pathetic faith. Full disclosure, I have tried every type of faith I just described. I have put each one on. Some felt cozy, filling my heart with a false sense of security. Some felt restrictive. I instinctively knew something was wrong. Some made me feel like a spiritual super star, yet I was missing that key ingredient, the fuel, that propels a faithful follower. I was missing humility. I determined my faith combos, my lists and my us-versus-others were getting in my way. Realizing my "faith" was not launching me into His inside out, upside down kingdom, my heart began to hunger and thirst for A Faith Worth Having. So I began my adventure to find a gritty, remarkable, astounding, quiet, daring, leaping faith.

If you have never read a book about faith, about God, about Jesus, I hope you continue reading listening for God's gentle whispers of truth. If you are discouraged, I hope you hear your One and Only calling to you. If you are faithful and just needing some encouragement, I hope you hear your cheerleading Father celebrating the hard, beautiful choices you are making.

To all of you, as you read on, it is my hope and my prayer you find your Faith Worth Having.

Let these words flow over you

Seek God's wholeness, His holy otherness. Hurry toward true, reputable authentic, noble compelling grace. Find grace through praising Him. The most beautiful praise is a recipe for life giving happiness whether found in full hands or in empty. Drink from the chalice of life refreshingly hearty, filled with mercy cascading into the deep waters of our soul. Live each moment peaceful, joyous and full of love. Find God nearby. See the waving colored banners praising His name. God turns the tide and raises the victory flag torn from battles fought and won. He swings wide open His marvelous gates to hear victory shouts from above the chaos as triumphant songs ring out in jubilation. Our victories are His song, a toast to our magnificent, spectacular, tender and close God. An overflowing cup of salvation exceeds our expectations as glory pours from immutable grace and flows like a river with a transcendent current carrying us onto eternity. All the left behind, the overlooked, the underneath, the looked past, the least of these are victorious at last. A bonanza of hallelujahs ring out as we stand bathed in His love, His never fails, never quits, never falls away, love. Aromas call, calling us to be engulfed by the sweet smelling sacrifice of thanksgiving. We fall before the One and Only, the mysterious, the untamed, the abounding in generosity, never late, strong champion breathing out the truth to the thousands, cheering gloriously, rejoicing with thunderous applause. We enter with adoring praise, dancing to a new tune, living free and living full. Early one sun drenched day, just barely visible, falling like the morning dew we shine, bounce and reflect His glory refreshing all in sight.

Give glory to the One and Only.

Amen

CHAPTER 2

Lists, Bargains and Whispers

We are people of action. We want to do something! We pray "show me what to do to keep everything as perfect as this broken world will allow." God has given us story after story to reveal His heart and He has spoken through many authors. We seem to be drawn toward clear answers, right and wrong, black and white and do this and don't do that. Are we are attempting to build our perfect forever home right here on the third rock from the sun? Are we trying to create a spiritual safety net around our wish-would-last home. Protecting the gravity bound homestead, we enlist our list of dos and don'ts. These lists can go on and on. Most of us keep our lists with little effort. We invented our list. We've created them out our value systems and our ideas of what God wants. Much our lists can come from what looks good on the outside. Following a set of rules, even inspired rules does not protect from hard moments and cannot repair the separation between you and God.

Created to pull us toward God, our lists of dos and don'ts are also often things that keep us out of trouble. These lists in no way guarantee horrific times won't come upon us and engulf us or those we love. They don't make us superior. Our lists do not guarantee that those we love won't suffer loss, live with a broken heart or be crushed by this shattered and dysfunctional world. Ironically, the things we do for God or don't do can become a source of personal pride. If we'll do our very best, if we follow all of the "Dos" and "Don'ts," then God will have to take care of me and mine. We begin to create our cosmic equation. We believe there is a balance between our failures and God's fixes-His protection for us and our loved ones. We work at this balance. With this agreement in mind, we are willing to give God more of us, our families, our wants and our wishes. And though we may not say it out loud, we believe as we mature as we give more to God, then He is obligated, yes obligated to bless us.

Obligated!?! We believe the God of the universe is somehow obligated to protect us. He is required to fix all the pot holes, remove all the detours and to pave our road to complete fulfillment and constant joy. We are asking Him to bless the good things. The spiritual things we know will please Him. So, God should take care of us, right? We are following His rule book. If we believe we have some special arrangement with the mountain maker, ocean tamer, sky creator, God of the universe, then a deep faith isn't needed in our everyday life. When our frail faith is challenged by heart-aches, we falsely believe we didn't fulfill our end of the bargain. Inside our disorienting pain, we might think we are being punished or need correction.

Putting ourselves in The Almighty's shoes we know how we would rule planet earth, right? If God would just put us in charge, everything would be fair and equal. Life would make complete sense with no surprises. No one would suffer loss. Life would be lived out in perfect harmony even the top of the food chain lion would lay down with the defenseless sweet lamb. Oh wait, I am describing the way it was supposed to be before a quick snack from a forbidden tree. I am describing what is to come. I am looking forward to the new earth when the old things have passed away. There is a beginning to our story and an end. We need to remember we are living smack in the middle. We also need to remember we are not the center of the story. And, we are not "helping out" an author experiencing writer's block. (Proverbs 19:21) "We humans keep brainstorming options and plans, (I would add our lists dos, don'ts, our cosmic bargain and ideas for others) but God's purpose prevails." When you truly think about your capacity to live in humility, to extend grace and to put others before yourself, it clears up the fog of over confidence. When you think of the poor decisions you have made, it is absolutely ridiculous to believe you or I are ever in a position to fix even the smallest trouble of those we love.

We are not the Author of life, yet we do have free will, choice and years to influence both for good and for bad. We can grow and change, but we did not create this world and all its inhabitants. Even though we often act like we are running the show or at the very least we are living large in the center ring, we are not. Sometimes our world is reeling out of control from choices we have made. Ready for an attitude adjustment? Observe nature for an afternoon and God's overwhelming creative ability will knock us back into our proper place. Even His creation of the tiniest, of least of these, boggles our minds. Taking a small sample of God's creative work, we can be astonished by the intricacies and the variety throughout. Who thinks to create over twenty-two thousand species of ants? Did we come up with the crazy combo of a long neck, long thin legs and massive mid section feathers on a non-flying bird that can run at up to about forty-three mph?? Who designs fifty-four species of marine fishes that look like floating horses? Get this little twist for fun, the male seahorse carries the baby fish ponies. If this were true in humans, our population would have died out years ago?!? That is just a small sample of the amazing, astonishing, remarkable, incredible types of creatures that God has created. Mind-blowing everyday nature puts us back as the one created not the creator. Remembering our place and our humble beginning is a good place to begin. We are not God's partner, His co-pilot or a heavenly helper. Newsflash, we began as dirt. We do not have the power to add one thing to God's magnificent path He craved out for each of us. Can we conclude we need to step out of our grandiose, self-created spot-light and humbly kneel before the creator of the magnificent rainbow, Grand Canyon and the leaf cutting ant?

If we are to stand on our knees, if we are to change, if we are to move toward A Faith Worth Having, then we must accept three simple, yet profound life changing truths. In order to discover this faith-altering-truth, I had to go deep. I needed to scour several theological statements, dive into a number of doctrinal truths and pour over many biblical commentaries. I read several religious books and articles. I created and deconstructed complex scholarly thoughts that sparked many debates and filled hours of discussion. A teaching pastor would work hard to explain the multifaceted ideas I uncovered. I worked and worked to find the core, the hub-the center of faith. Finally nearing completion, I used biblical exegesis *"gazoontite"* and hermeneutics (isn't that a character from the Munster's???). Here we go. Are you ready for the deep, serious, powerful and amazing truth I discovered? Ready for the foundational truths that when deeply understood changes your life's trajectory?

Life is Hard. God is Good. Heaven is Sure.

These three simple truths are the anchors, the concrete footings, the foundation of A Faith Worth Having. They are our plumb line and our GPS for having a healthy spiritual life. Keeping these at the forefront of our thinking, near our heart will help us make sense of any situation this life throws at us. These three simple truths allow us to be at our best when life is at its worst. Boil it down further into one to word TRUST. Trust when life is hard. Trust that God is always a Good God. Trust in our futures because a Good God holds them. Trust because Heaven is Sure. There is complex truth and there is simple truth. Simple is all my heart can do when life falls apart. If we have struggled to lay it all down, then we need to take a small, yet reorienting, first step. Stop. Stop moving and listen. Stopping our whirling life and becoming a better listener will lead us to a place where we can finally see how to change so that our faith can begin to grow.

God is clear. He is not present in our demanding with a gale force wind ripping through the trees and the rocks. He is not present in our frustration that seems to shake everything around us nor is He present in our passionate pleading that burns up everything in sight. Listen, quiet your heart and listen for a gentle whisper. Listen. God is in the whisper. Often, we are so busy telling God what to do or complaining about our perceived terrible circumstances that only our own words ring in our own ears. Only when we strip it all away and let the quiet fill the air, can we hear the whisper. Listen, He is in the whisper. "I am here. I see you. I know my dear one. I know the pain you are in. I am here as near as your own heart beat. I will never leave you. I am as close as each breath. Trust that I love you." Let His presence fall like rain. He is ever present, ever close. He is in the whisper.

Life is Hard. God is Good. Heaven is Sure.

Let these words wash over you

Quiet. Listen. Know God wants so much more for us than we can ever imagine. Beyond being our best when life is at its worst, God desires for His loved ones to live out joyously with complete abandonment in our worship, in our prayers and in our relationship with Him. Joy in All circumstances. Deep, deep all encompassing love for God and others. Trust with utter dependence and authentic vibrant love with the ability to say yes when everything is on the line when everything we care about is at stake. Live so the least of these gets a hero's welcome. Uncover who or what we are living for by retracing our steps. Dig beyond this discovery and push toward trust. Push toward an authentic relationship with God. Live out loud. Live with arms open. Hear celebrations standing on your knees listening for His whisper. Bravely lift your face with cheeks stained by falling tears and abandon it all for the One and Only leaving no one behind. All are welcome and deeply loved. All are wrapped up in His joy not temporary happiness but His unfathomable subterranean joy.

Amen

CHAPTER 3

Life is Hard

Life is Hard: Brutally hard, grueling, heart-wrenching, children get sick, awful, devastating, disappointing, disorienting, crushing, children go hungry, shattering, senseless, cataclysmic, overwhelming, the good so often get run over, deeply unfair, broken, cruel, violent **Hard**.

When we sugar-coat, ignore, pretend life isn't so bad or believe we can outsmart the brokenness that plagues others, we deny a vital truth that underlines our need for a Faith Worth Having. Life is Hard. We can numb, distract and discount this truth. When we do this, we no longer need God's help, God's presence or God's Son. There is a book in the middle of the Bible called the Psalms. It is a book of prayers that were originally sung at worship gatherings. If you have never read them, you will not find pat answers or happy platitudes. There are some beautiful pictures of God's love and His power. There are also some raw depictions of Life is Hard. In fact after reading several psalms, it may feel as if an old pipe has burst gushing down a shower of sorrow and brokenness. Over and over through-out the one-hundred and fifty Psalms the writers paint some truly horrific images. Here is just a very small sampling.

Psalm 42:9
⁹ "Sometimes I ask God, my rock-solid God,
　 "Why did you let me down?
Why am I walking around in tears,
　 harassed by enemies?"

Psalm 40:11-12
¹¹⁻¹² "Now GOD, don't hold out on me,
　 don't hold back your passion.
Your love and truth

are all that keeps me together.
When troubles ganged up on me,
   a mob of sins past counting,
I was so swamped by guilt
   I couldn't see my way clear.
More guilt in my heart than hair on my head,
   so heavy the guilt that my heart gave out."

Psalm 38:5-8

[5-8] "cuts in my flesh stink and grow maggots
   because I've lived so badly.
And now I'm flat on my face
   feeling sorry for myself morning to night.
All my insides are on fire,
   my body is a wreck.
I'm on my last legs; I've had it—
   my life is a vomit of groans."

Psalm 38:17-18

[17-18] "I'm on the edge of losing it—
   the pain in my gut keeps burning.
I'm ready to tell my story of failure,
   I'm no longer smug in my sin."

A few of my favorite phrases from these scriptures are "Why am I walking around in tears?" "Swamped by guilt." "Edge of losing it." My personal favorite is "My life is a vomit of groans." This Life is Hard is at times unbearably bone-crushing hard.

How often do we ask this question, "Why do bad things happen to good people?" In Proverbs, the book in the Bible right after the book of Psalms, there is a wise saying that states, "Without warning your life can turn upside down, and who knows how or when it might happen?" (Proverbs 24:22). That's one Proverb, one drop of wisdom, surely there are plenty of verses that affirm us and encourage us. Yes, there are a tremendous amount of verses that affirm God's unlimited grace, His everlasting love and His forever mercy, and yet, the cold hard truth is this Life is Hard.

It is not only the big challenges that make life hard. It is also the everyday stuff, the daily grind, a grating routine, a very small relentless pain or searing ache. It's like walking on tiny bits of broken glass. Those irritants cause us to walk gingerly as if on eggshells. We limp through each moment. The smallest of things can bring life to a halt. The surprisingly razor-sharp pain of stepping on a tiny thorn stops all progress as we singularly focus on getting relief.

I call these tiny, mighty life altering sorrows a *Heavy lift of a Small Burden.*

- Chronic pain
- On-going health challenges
- Frustrating or strained marriages
- Irritating or mean co-workers
- Concern over a struggling child/teenager/adult child
- Chronic fatigue
- Money concerns
- Under employment

This list goes on and on. The pain or the aching from a heavy lift of a small burden is just as taxing as a major life explosion. We can become utterly exhausted from this seemly small struggle. Adding to the challenge, we bury or minimize this pain and receive little if any support for such a small everyday trial. When life crashes into us, for most of us, our friends and family gather quickly. They call. They text. A few may send a card, send flowers or even stop by. Email lists are compiled to help with meals, chores and car pools. Friends are there to shoulder the confusion of no answers. If we are truly blessed, someone may offer to come and just sit with us as we travel the darkest road trying to digest the hardest answer of all. "It's back. There is nothing we can do but try and make him comfortable." Life stops. Pain envelops, loved ones rally and a heart wrenching journey begins. When life crashes into us, we live each day in the profound bottomless moments of sadness. We need to realize the everyday annoyances, a heavy lift of a small burden, wear upon our souls, our minds and our bodies. These small everyday burdens can wear us down to the very nub. Something little, something insignificant, an everyday part of life can create unyielding pressure.

What kind of pressure can a small burden produce? A familiar tale can give us some insights. Alexander the lion had stepped on a tiny thorn. He thought it was insignificant until he tried to run, to walk and even hobbling was uncomfortable. No longer was it small or insignificant.

This little burden, this little thorn was ruining his life. Before the Lion's thorn injury, he trapped a timid mouse named Oliver. The thorn wasn't tiny to the mouse. Oliver, desperate to save his own fur, astutely used the power of this little thorn to save his life. This insignificant thorn was now Oliver's only hope! A tiny thorn became his way of escape. Oliver had to thank his wife for making him take that online class "Thorn Extractions 101." Removing the tiny, insignificant thorn completely changed two lives forever. Now rid of the sharp pain Alexander was free to run, to gallop and to walk. The lion spared Oliver and was in his debt forever. A little, insignificant thorn immediately reversed Oliver's fortune, because he now had a friend at the top of the food chain. Alexander, the magnificent beast who ruled the plains of Africa, was brought down by the enormous power of an tiny thorn!

Little doesn't always mean little. If we live in a little pain all the time, then we need to realize what a toll that takes on our emotional, our physical and our spiritual lives. The daily heavy lift of a small burden is often under estimated. We think this not a big deal. "It's just chronic migraines. It's just stress at work. It's just fatigue from insomnia." It is just. This "just" is part of our daily life, part of our journey and part of our story. Yet, we are worn out, stretched to the limit and overwhelmed by the unrelenting pressure of this little challenge, this "just" a heavy lift of a small burden. Life is Hard. Sometimes a heavy lift of a small burden is what makes life hard.

The pain in our lives can come from the inside or the outside. Things are quickly and completely out of our control. Seen the news? Kept up with the weather? It is marked by devastation from too much heat, too much rain or too little heat, too little rain. Kept current with of the political systems? Some are dysfunctional. Some are oppressive. And some are dysfunctional and oppressive. Let's face it big or small, near or far, inside or outside, our world is broken. We live in a truly shattered world today with little chance for change. Life is hard. Our stomachs turn in knots when we see or hear about the injustices. It seems school shootings happen often. Drivers awake over twenty four hours crash sending innocent lives to the hospital and morgue. Childhood cancer, two words that should never ever be placed next to each other, has become all too common. Our world is often so broken we cannot make sense out of any of it. A joyous moment "We're pregnant" collapses in deep grief when at the next appointment "no heart beat" is whispered. These moments are disorientating to say the least.

This place we call home for the duration of our earthly existence is filled with thousands, upon thousands of ruined lives and overwhelmed families with broken hearts and devastated dreams. Wonderfully good, kind, loving people are reduced to rubble. Life crashes into to us and we stand seemly helpless to cope. We feel we have so little control. So, we spend time simply numbing the pain. If life has not crashed into us, then it has crashed into those we love. They have been devastated by a list of diseases that fill volumes of medical records and we watch powerlessly as our love ones bravely battle. The medical treatments meant to heal can be even crueler than the sickness itself. Occasionally, to our complete and utter exasperation, they courageously fight a battle they will never win. We watch helplessly as those we love more than life itself wither and fade away. It is as if our flesh is being torn away as we are forced to say a final good-bye. Unfortunately, the list goes on and on from injustice, difficult circumstances, fractured relationships to damaged and ruined lives. We cannot outsmart this etched-in-stone truth that our Life is Hard

We bargain, connive and work every situation. Using the tools of our day, the right school, the right friends and the right job, we position ourselves to live on top of the mountain towering above all the sickness, all the brokenness and all the hard times that plague most people. Like a sea gull soaring above the waves, we calmly outwit all the messy without even getting sea spray in our eyes. What do we forfeit by numbing, ignoring or running from the truth that Life is Hard? If life were easy and manageable, then we wouldn't need God even our amazingly awe inspiring, good God. If our life is perfect-ish here, then why pursue A Faith Worth Having? Without the cold hard facts that Life is Hard, we live a blind, deaf and dumb existence. If we only focus on God is Good and Heaven is Sure, then we are only two-thirds of the way to A Faith Worth Having. Imagine, we have just received a bar stool sent from IKEA. The problem is we only have two legs of a three legged stool. Who doesn't call IKEA and demand the other leg? Without that third leg Life is Hard, we will never be able to stand. Forget about our eternal contribution. Forget about what God intended our life to bear. When we ignore, numb and create our own reality, we live by our self-created truth. We build our life around our idea of justice and fairness. We believe "bad things only happen to bad people." So, we spend our time avoiding "bad" and trying to be "good."

Have you met Jesus? He triumphantly waded into messiness and unspeakable brokenness of those around Him. Those who have surrendered to the forever love of Jesus know our story does not end in despair! We know Life is Hard can be an authentic depiction of our life right now, but it is not our ending. Remember we are living in the **middle** of the story. The truth is Life is Hard and the truth is God is Good. Life is only worth living because of a good God. We need the truth God is Good if we are to survive our difficult moments.

We need the truth God is Good if we are going to live our best possible life. Life is Hard and God is Good.

It is my prayer that as you read you feel His encouragement. If the words in this chapter sing true to your ears, then take some time to hear from the ultimate encourager. These verses are found in the book of Psalms.

Psalm 52:8-9
[8] "And I'm an olive tree,
    growing green in God's house.
I trusted in the generous mercy
    of God then and now.
[9] I thank you always
    that you went into action.
And I'll stay right here,
    your good name my hope,
    in company with your faithful friends."

If the concepts and ideas have made you question your views on spirituality, then it is my prayer that you find Him in the simplicity of these small yet powerful truths. Life is Hard. God is Good. Heaven is Sure.

Soak in these words as they cascade into a rushing river

Flourish and thrive surrounding ourselves with the gracious, sweet, never late, always there God. Let His truth hem us in and wash over us. May His love be our covering, our cloak. Feel the warmth of His affection, His kindness and His everlasting welcome. Embrace longed-for, long-awaited unwarranted grace. Feel His delightful, pleasing, refreshing appreciation. Seek Jesus' the same, never wavering and forever arms. Stand open with our heart now ready to jump at a life without fear. Live in the midst of broken, heart-wrenching and shattered lives. Triumphant Jesus walks nearer to us than our heart beat. He paints our world in hues of laughter, splashes of unspeakable joy, primary colors of love, waves of hope and a wash of peace. Follow Him. Follow close. Try to match Him step for step. Placing our feet inside His foot prints, travel this exquisitely wild journey. A journey filled with ups and very difficult downs. This journey brings joys, amazing joys and deep life altering sadness. This journey leads to the greatest prize to Jesus Himself. Even in our brokenness hold on to the One and Only knowing life has little meaning away from Him. Live like we know we living in the middle, not the beginning and definitely not the ending. Live in the middle clinging to the God of the Universe the creator of daisies, fruit flies and the platypus. He will hold on to us as we grab hold of Him. Rest in Him. He is mine and you are His.

Amen

CHAPTER 4

God is Good

God is Good: Amazing, spectacular, awesome, healing where there was no longer any hope, suddenly spring, when at last, showering blessings upon blessings, overflowing, as close as each heartbeat, shiver with awe, joy beyond joy, a love that's higher, wider, deeper and closer than imagined, Holy and wholly other, beyond our comprehension, grand, overwhelming, stunning, out of this world. **Good**.

Why a focus on God is Good? This seems to be so obvious for those who have walked with God for years. Why the reminder? Why do we need to keep this in the forefront of our thinking? Here is the truth clearly stated in a letter written to the Christians in Rome from book of Romans. As you read, put the mature believer, someone who has been a Christian for many years, in place of name Israel.

Romans 9:30-33. "How can we sum this up? All the people who didn't seem interested in what God was doing actually embraced what God was doing as he straightened out their lives. And Israel (mature believer), who seemed so interested in reading and talking about what God was doing, missed it. How could they miss it? **Instead of trusting God, they took over.** They were absorbed in what they themselves were doing. They were so absorbed in their 'God projects' that they didn't notice God right in front of them, like a huge rock in the middle of the road. And so they stumbled into him and went sprawling. Isaiah (again!) gives us the metaphor for pulling this together: 'Careful! I've put a huge stone on the road to Mount Zion,

> a stone you can't get around. But the stone is me (Jesus)! If you're looking for me, you'll find me on the way, not in the way"

Could the boulder blocking our way to living out real, authentic, make-a-difference faith be Jesus? Are we running our lives without much interaction with Jesus? He calls us to Himself. He desires us **not** what we bring to Him. He wants you and He wants me. Why the struggle to believe God is Good? The frustrating fact is that many of us wrestle with a discouraging truth. If God is Good, then why does He allow me or to my loved ones to hurt? "God will cure this disease, right?" "He will help me figure out my marriage. He will keep divorce off the table." This is how we usually pray to the author of life, omnipresent, omnipotent God, "God answer my prayer exactly as have I laid it out and answer that prayer right now!" I have wasted years praying this way.

When we take over, direct the outcomes, effectively leaving Jesus out, we minimize Life is Hard putting ourselves in the driver's seat attempting to control every outcome. If life isn't so bad, so hard, then we don't really need to rely on a good God, right? We have this life by the tail. We work most of our days protecting our loved ones and fixing everything we see. Getting to know our God personally isn't a priority. We're so busy fixing everything and everyone that we have little time to spend with God. We don't say this out loud, but this is how we live. We believe we know what is best. We desire that God quickly answers each of our prayers. We lay out the answers we want. We wait for Him to follow our instructions. We are shattered if the answer we petitioned for is not given. Sometimes it is as if we are asking for three wishes from our heavenly genie. When life crashes into us, it is serious. We are in true pain. We have nowhere else to turn. We are lost. We are begging for help and the issues we face can be life threatening. God is still Good. In the midst of everything going wrong God is still Good. When an answer doesn't come or the answer is the worst possible news God is still Good. We have to lay down our preconceived notions of what good looks like and look to God Himself. Look to all He is doing and has done. Look for His presence in the everyday.

If you old enough to remember the 1939 classic the Wizard of Oz, you remember it was shown only once a year in late October. If you remember when there were only eight TV channels, you may also remember being the remote. Yes, before Cable, smart TV and Netflix, before the universal remote, when called upon, I was the remote. I can still hear my Father yelling, "Change the channel and then get back from the T.V." As a child sitting on the floor, not too close to the TV, I remember that heart stopping, catch your breath moment, as Dorothy steps out of her black and white, slightly run down, dingy farm house into a vibrant dazzling layer upon layer wash of Technicolor. It was a stunningly delicious feast for my eyes when Dorothy entered Oz

Just like the colors of Oz, God crafted a vibrant world to be seen daily in the beauty and intricacies of nature. God is Good. Have you ever considered the plethora of the colors you are immersed in daily? Pinks, blue, violet, gold, shimmering almost transparent yellow and those are just the colors of one sunset in late spring. Have you ever considered you could have lived in black and white your entire life? God the ultimate creator fashioned our world and eyes so we would see so much color that we would take it for granted. Here in the majestically unseen these "taken for granted" aspects of our world God's goodness calls to us. Have you ever considered the beauty of in each color? Can you hear Him in the pinks and blues, in the purples and yellows, in the oranges and the reds? God is Good. God is calling us in the rainbow of colors we see every day.

Touch is another "taken for granted" part of life we probably never truly think about. We can feel the warmth of a hug, the comfort of holding a loved one's hand, the pure sweetness of a gentle kiss. We can touch. We can feel. A caress, a cuddle, a hug, an embrace, a gentle pat, a squeeze, God is good. These two "taken for granted" everyday senses, color and touch, are megaphones that announce our God is Good. These two majestically unseen parts of everyday life reveal a good God. Attempting to list His sweet, magnificent good would be like trying to count the sand crystals on the beach or numbering the stars in the heavens. Picture a white sandy beach. See the hypnotic rhythm of each ocean wave as it daily caress the shore. As each wave laps, now try and count each sand crystal, crushed shell or broken rock. Impossible. Later, the sun fades behind the horizon. Streaks of pinks, yellow, and blues swallow the sky. The sun winks goodbye as it finally slips away. Darkness arrives. Now, take in the breathtaking beauty of the pitch dark night sky pieced only by tiny white lights as far as the eye can see. Counting each twinkling star dancing throughout the universe would be unthinkable. Every shiny sand crystal in the ocean and each glimmering star at night bare witness and cry out to the unfathomable, amazing, goodness of our beautiful and mighty God.

One final everyday example is God's goodness placed inside the family. Another "taken for granted" is the gift of doing life with the forever love of mom and dad, sisters and brother, nieces and nephews. Don't get me started on the breath-taking beauty of a new born cradled in his mama's arms with a proud papa looking on. God's good is the privilege of personally raising our children. For many parents, God in His goodness grants them the honor of feeling every emotion. Pride and delight, mixed in with a little sorrow, fills each heart as loved ones walk across a simple wooden bridge receiving a High School diploma. God's fingerprints are all over the absolute and utter bittersweet joy of watching our greatest love continue his or her journey. Every minute of family joy, warmth, humor, sleepless night, miles spent in the car, to and from lessons or practices, fun, comfort, correction, frustration, contentment, every trial and every blessing invites us to see that families were created by our heavenly Father to increase life's significance and give us unspeakable joy. God is Good.

Many of us accept this truth that God is Good, but we pull away from this truth rather than leaning in. We falsely believe a good God could only love those who are good. Our immature love loves only what is similar. We love ourselves first than we love those who seem like us next. We can live a lifetime and never love those different from us. God doesn't see the differences. Pick any life circumstance and the truth is there but the graces of God go you and go I. No one really knows what each life path involves. *"Everyone may not be good, but there's always something good in everyone. Never judge anyone shortly because every saint has a past and every sinner has a future."*— Oscar Wilde

We can also falsely believe we need to get it all together before we will experience God's goodness in our lives. The flaw in this thinking can be refuted by watching our parent's love. Healthy, loving parents love all the time. Yes, they can become disappointed, even angry at their child's life choices, but they never stop loving him or loving her. Can you imagine your three year old saying, "Let me get my preschool duckies in a row, then I will come with open chubby toddler arms ready to trust you and your love." Parents are deeply in love with their children no matter the circumstances, the challenges and even the heartaches. We push God away, "God, wait till I am better, wait for me to get it all together, then I will come to you." We put on God what we feel, but God is the ultimate Daddy. He loves because we are His true family. He doesn't need our performance to grease the wheels to find a way to love us. God loves you. God loves me. God is Good and He has loved us from the beginning.

If we won't or can't see that God is Good, then we live working and performing with one foot in the kingdom and the other foot firmly in our world. We live trying to please God and trying to please ourselves. We don't try to pursue Him, love Him and simply be with Him. We perform for God living in a palpable state of fear of failure. We live in constant worry of messing up. An inward focus paralyzes us so that we never live out His life and never give away anything of value to those around us. We never make our forever kingdom impact. We are hot air escaping from a balloon. We live luke-warm uselessly trying to give what we "think" God wants from us. God is Good. Without this truth we are simply living a good life and trying to do the right thing for here and now. God is Good gives our lives perspective, grit, purpose and strength so that we can be our best when life is at its worst. The truth is Life is Hard. And, the truth is God is Good.

God's Goodness can be seen in His light searing through the darkness. However dark, His light can pierce it. Jesus came to be that light that brings us lovingly to the Heavenly Father. God loves us so much. He wants you and He wants me. He wants us. He wants all of us. Our guilt, our shame, all our reasons we are not worthy are completely wiped clean by one selfless act. The ultimate self-sacrificing act is Jesus dying on a wooden cross for you and for me. These hands willingly stretched wide nailed for our transgressions. These hands stained with blood cleanse the darkest offense. These hands bearing the scars make everything whole. These hands break every chain and conquer every fear. These hands created you and created me. These hands cheer us on and calling us home. Firmly planted on forever soil because of the One I am following, this carpenter turned teacher, turned master, turned ultimate sacrifice for my indulgences, my failures, my crummy choices, my guilt and my shame. Jesus came for one reason. The Ultimate Sacrifice stood in my place. I am clean because God is Good.

Spend some time in His Presence

Grotesquely beaten, nails pounded. Side wounded. Death celebrates. Days pass. Morning breaks. The tomb is empty. He is risen. He is risen indeed. Death defeated is no more. Tears wiped away forever. Every worthless deed, every shame, every confession, every crummy choice vanish forever. Every ugly act wiped clean by the blood of this gentle warrior. Jesus washes all our self-centered grime away. God's undeniable goodness summed up in one sentence. God loves me and God loves you. Every quick heart beat, goose bump, nervous butterfly as we seek His presence reveals God's breath covering our dust to dust existence. His love is an everlasting, always present, never late, ready to catch us kind of love. More than we ever expected is this love. It is the purest love. Hurry toward this love that holds all things together. Rush into His presence to drink from the never-ending fountain of adoration, mercy and thanksgiving. Lean into Him and wait with joy. Serve with charity and soar to colossal heights. Standing on the foundation God loves you. The ear maker, soul keeper, finger print designer, heart tender and life creator wants you and He wants me. Standing on our knees we raise arms to worship the One and Only. Our maker, defender, redeemer, restorer and transporter calls to us. When in our darkest dark and from our deepest hole, call out to Him who bandages each wound and heals every hurt. The gentle warrior king stands ready. He runs to you. Simply, call out to Him. God is Good. Every enemy is defeated. Jesus has come.

Amen

Chapter 5

Heaven is Sure

Heaven is sure. In His presence forever, tears are wiped away and gone forever, healing, safe, comfort, whole, happy, contentment, blissful, joyful, awesome, a real place where celebrations with our loved ones await, where our choices matter, our lives go on and on, all questions are answered or those questions no longer need to be asked, our destination after faithful battles and victory at last, where we see the face of God and worship Him in person, everlasting bliss, resting in His forever arms. Home finally home. **Heaven.**

No eye has seen what God has planned for us. This life is not the end. There is more. We believe God has gone ahead of us and prepared a place for us. It is strange to think that we have another home waiting for us. I used to joke with friends where our heavenly homes might be. Who would live next door to whom? I think the perfect home we have tried to create here in our cul-de-sac waits for us on the other side. We think we can create the perfect life and have perfect relationships here and now. Naively, when it all shatters we can't figure out why. After that fateful bite of forbidden fruit, life became unpredictably troublesome. It is impossible to have perfect relationships with those we love. Every relationship we have is contaminated. Every relationship has an expiration date. Here on earth they all end.

Death was an add-on. It is something we were never meant to experience. Every death like every life is unique. Death is not something we can control. We can't put it off or be shielded from it. Death is a real part of our lives. Grief comes as we watch those we love fade. Grief comes because a separation looms. Death or dying is like that dark alley no one ever enters, yet every time we walk by, there is an uneasy feeling. We cannot put death off or pretend it only happens after we have lived a long happy and healthy life. Death can surprise us. It almost sneaks up on us. Wham! Our life will never be the same. God meets us in our grief and our sorrow. We are changed as we grieve and celebrate. Finally, we say the ultimate goodbye. We are changed when we watch all our loved ones, our dearest ones, grieve. After traveling several roads to places we never thought we'd see and experiencing the deepest sorrow, we say the hardest goodbye. We are never the same.

Recently, I saw the musical Les Mis produced at Grace Church in Noblesville, Indiana. Because of my involvement and because it was an amazing show, I saw it several times. What struck me was how we hunger see a glimpse of heaven. The musical ends with a glorious triumphant song. Every character stood triumphantly singing their hearts out. Audiences stood to their feet, and the applause roared. Most of the characters had died during the show. Even the lead dies at the end, but what brought audiences to their feet was not just the soaring music and it soared. What brought audiences to their feet was not just the glorious, amazing victorious singing and it was amazingly glorious. No, what I believe brought people to their feet was the sight of those we just witnessed dying now standing center stage singing out this truth. Life can go on. Celebratory, jubilant, exuberant life goes on. Heaven is Sure. We need to see, to hear and to tell others that Heaven is Sure. This fact, this truth, is something that affects all we do in this life. The truth, life does go on, needs to be in the forefront of our everyday thinking. Because we are earth bound, this truth Heaven is Sure must be front and center. It must be a part of all we do.

Field of Dreams and Titanic are two other movies audiences couldn't seem to get enough of. Why? Resurrection scenes are a big part of both movies. In an out-of-this-world everyday moment, Kevin Costner's character runs out onto a baseball field to play catch with his dad even though his father had died. Heaven is Sure. From Titanic, who can forget that picture of the lead characters, Rose and Jack, walking up the grand staircase lined with all the people we just witnessed freezing to death in the icy, unforgiving, dark ocean water. We watched the young couple dance in a beautifully restored world. All is well, and death is no more. Heaven is Sure is a part of our story too. We don't seem to want to talk about it. We need to talk about it. Others need to see it in us and hear it from us. We forget how hungry they are to hear this truth.

Death is not the final good-bye only a temporary separation. The tomb was empty. Death, where is your sting? We grieve deeply, but we grieve only for a short while until the veil is lifted. Having stood by the caskets of many an "out of order" death, the comfort that heaven brings is immeasurable. It is the unseen truth that we must trust with every breath we take. Standing in the shadow of the final injustice, love taken, we fill our lungs and exhale. We believe there will be air to take that next breath and so begins our journey back to life. We also believe death has been utterly defeated. It is this truth that holds us together, literally holds onto us, when everything we love shatters into tiny pieces. It is our anchor as we watch those tiny pieces dissolve into chaos. We can be completely devastated, wrecked, yet in these spirit-crushing moments we gasp for life-giving breath. Like the warmth of spring, a tender strength begins to take root, we remember Heaven is Sure. We somehow find the strength to go on. We find the strength to get out of bed the next morning. And so it goes. We just do the next thing. We can move forward even when our life is splintered and completely unrecognizable.

Life is hard. God is good. Heaven is sure. The truth is God wants **more for** us than we can even imagine! We are all at a place where God wants us to move toward trusting Him more. We are all transformations waiting to happen. We are all rescue stories. We are all a redeemed transformation, rescue story in action. We all know life can and does crash into us. I believe God takes us from mature to complete through the Life is Hard moments. Being at our best when life is at its worst, we Stand on our Knees and live out A Faith Worth Having. If we sugar-coat the hard times and try to protect ourselves from never feeling the bitter cold brokenness within our circle of loved ones, then we will never need A Faith Worth Having. Are we going to trust in ourselves, our plans, our purposes and our list's of do's and don'ts? If we never look at the last chapters of our story or the stories of those we love, then we become tempted to make our own heaven on earth. We live for today. Well-resourced responsible people live for their future trusting their financial planning, retirement accounts and their raining day savings. We live out our lives trapped behind the huge wall surrounding us called the calendar. Programmed into our smart phones, not a day goes by that we don't interact with the tyranny of now. With our feet thick in the settled concrete buried underneath the urgent, we cannot make even the slightest eternal impact. If we ignore the fact that this life ends, if we refuse to believe we go on and on and on, we will never be at our best when life is at its worst.

What about our forever? Could we give it all away? Can we die broke knowing wealth beyond our wildest dreams is just beyond the other side? Can we trust our future both here on earth and after this life to a good God? Feel like wrestling a little more? Spend some time wrestling with these questions. When life crashes into us how do we respond? Do you and I run to family, friends or experts? Do we fear we have failed if we are experiencing a Life is Hard season? Are we frustrated, unhappy and angry? Do we complain? Do we ask why? Why me? Why now? Why my family? Why me and mine? Why?

Are you and I trusting in "being good" to lead us through the Life is Hard moments? What is our spirituality anchored in? Do you and I cling to the faith of those we love? Do you and I turn toward God crying out in complete, utter dependence? Or do we complain, second guess and scheme a way to fix things or at the very least try and force things to go our way? Can we let go of the God we created? Can we yield to the Creator who has the right to send us through whatever experience He chooses? Do we believe God is present in our circumstances? How does our life exemplify our beliefs? Do we believe Life is Hard, God is Good and Heaven is Sure? What is keeping us from a Faith Worth Having?

Proverbs 24:10 "If you fall to pieces in crisis there wasn't much of you in the first place."

Life is Hard. God is Good. Heaven is Sure

Listen for the whisper.

Make a run for God we won't regret it. We'll have God's more-than-enough. We will be drenched in His affectionate satisfaction painting grace graffiti on the walls, fences and tunnels of your life. We'll have His Word, the best home cooking ever. When everything in life falls apart, it's put back together by star-flinging fingers. Travel every road tested by His righteous revelation, held firm in His hand and caressed by gentle love. Live out a titanic purpose with the exquisite splendor of a God-gripped life, living spacious and free, protected and safe. We'll have armloads of blessings, a God-given-edge and a secure future on the solid rock. Hope patiently, persistently, piercing the indifference by dancing to a God-revelation-tune as the years of our life ripen. Beauty and love chase after us day after day after day. Leap into our future secure in ever present arms, everlasting love, tranquility and overwhelming joy. Indescribable joys are waiting for us. Lay it down at the pierced feet of the most magnificent gentle king who gave His all so we could go on and on. To the Forgiver of our past, the Maker of our present and the Author of forever, let there be honor and glory forever and ever.

Amen

CHAPTER 6

The Ugly Truth

A recent phenomenon called Helicopter parenting smothers children with intense love and constant attention. There was a day when children were seen and not heard. In the not too distant past, children were allowed to roam. They were not restricted to their driveway and part of the cul-de-sac. Like herds of buffalo, they roamed freely throughout their entire neighborhoods. They also rode their bikes miles to and from their grammar schools. And they rode with the wind whipping through their hair riding without a helmet! In those days helmets were reserved for those crazy motorcycle daredevils like Evel Knievel. Of course, the most dangerous experience of a child's life happened almost daily by simply riding in the family car, unrestrained! I remember traveling in an old station wagon facing backward unbuckled just a few layers of metal between me and that semi racing past. I happily moved from seat to seat without a care in the world while huge tractor tailors nipped at our heels going seventy miles an hour.

Stating the obvious, times have changed. Safety is everywhere. We are bombarded daily with warning labels, buckle up, wear that bike helmet, choking hazard, alerts and alarms. Notifications tell us to be very, very careful. We are lured into thinking we can make a very safe and secure world. Maybe a better way to state our current environment is to say we work at being safe and value being secure. We live in an era where pushing of a few buttons on our phone gives us access to our homes. We can see if our widows are locked, temperature is set right and if our garage door has been accidently left open. My parents used the phone to call me at the neighbors, so I could run home to check and see if the garage door had been accidently left open. Having the power to connect, to check, to report and to video everything because of this little device we carry everywhere gives us a false sense of control and a false sense of security. We put our trust in "Set the alarm. Be on the lookout. Safety first. Remember safety first!" If we could, we'd create holy bubble wrap and wrap up everyone we love. Most of us hope and pray if tragedy does strike we will hold up well and that we are prepared for every conceivable outcome. We hope we will ready. We plan and push to be ahead of the game. But beneath the surface lies an etched-granite-truth stating we want control over our life. And our goal is simple to keep the brokenness and the pain far, far away from ourselves and our loved ones. Can we create a safe haven, an island for ourselves and loved ones, far, far from everything that is painful or dangerous?

Look just past Eden's perfect garden it is clear we were born into a desperately unsafe, broken world. From John 16:33 Jesus tells us we will have trouble. He doesn't say maybe. He doesn't say only a few have to worry. He doesn't say only those who make poor choices and those who really, really mess things up. Jesus states the truth. We (all of us) will have trouble. Yet, when trouble knocks we open the door and stand there like a deer in caught in the head lights. We're confused, shocked and disoriented. How can our safe-corner-of-the-world have problems, brokenness or troubles?

How do we move away from control freaks toward a deeper faith? How can we change from protecting our perfect happiness-now-and-always life. Stop then move. We need to stop gluing each shattered piece back in its original spot. We need to move toward accepting the hard. Do not miss this. This is not a retreat. This will take more blood, more sweat and more guttural strength than we can imagine. We are not giving in nor giving up. Before we can grow or change, we have to accept that **all** our human efforts to keep ourselves safe and our loved ones safe are worthless. This can be a terrifying truth for some. This is where authentic faith begins. We live in the post-perfection times. Eve offered. Adam ate. Sin entered and Life is Hard was born. Life has been forever changed. The horse is out of the barn. The milk is split. The cat is out of the bag. I am not sure why the cat was ever in the bag, but that cat is definitely OUT of the bag?!? We cannot go back to what God first imagined, but we can move into what God has prepared for us now and look forward to our perfect future in Him.

What keeps you from a strong, deep, sweet, real, never giving up on God but honest about the pain and the hurt kind of faith? What is keeping you from Standing on our Knees living out A Faith Worth Having? Remember that bargain with God? Take a hard look at how you do life. Can you concede that you have set up a cosmic bargain with the God of the universe? You may call God a force or universal power, but the bargain is the same. You'll do your best and God has to take care of you. God is now bound to care for you and for yours. You are willing to give God more of yourself, your lives, your wants and your wishes. You may not say it out loud, but you believe as you mature and as you give more to God, He'll have to protect you. He'll make you safe and bless you. "Yes God, You may have more of us, but in return we require not request, require Your protection and Your quick assistance. Thank you, Cosmic Creator of a Billion Stars, thanks a lot!"

Can we let go of the safe God we created? Can we yield to the unpredictable Creator who has every right to send us through whatever experience He chooses? No longer laying claim to our current path, can we let go? It is His right to take us in whatever direction He sees fit. Are we open to following this wildly, unpredictable, untamed God? Or do we serve a small, limited God? Is the Jesus we serve predictable and small? Is the Jesus we follow contained and sealed neatly packaged, frozen in a clear plastic container? Several years ago I was browsing in a Christian book store and I came across a Jesus toy action figure. It was the flannel graph version of Jesus I grew up with. He was dressed in His white robe with the blue sash. No cape but He did have three fish and five loaves. It seemed the toy maker was placing Jesus, the Sovereign Lord, God's One and Only son, in competition with Spiderman, Superman and the other caped crusaders to decide who is the most powerful!?! I had a ten minute dialogue with myself . How ridiculous! The sight of God incarnate hanging next to extra plastic animals for Noah's Ark, a plush musical lamb and a Bob and Larry Veggie Tales backpack makes no sense!?! Who creates a plastic Son of God then puts Him in a clear wrapper and places Him on a store shelf, absurd!?! Feeling fairly smug having voiced my justified indignation, I moved on hoping I had not accidentally offended someone shopping near me.

Later, it occurred to me have I ever taken my Jesus, my One and Only, refashioned Him into a small, plastic figure, then placed Him on a forgotten shelf? Do I try and make Jesus and God safe? Do I ever decide what Jesus can and cannot do? It is absurd to see the Creator of the universe on store shelf complete with the warning "Unsuitable for small children. Do not use with children under three. Choking hazard." Equally absurd is trying to minimize God or trying to control God, but it seems we can't help ourselves. We have zero control over what happens to others, zero control over our changing our world and adding to our dilemma we often have zero control ourselves. Unfortunately, controlling our life is our default mode. Our ideas, our plans and our perceived strengths hover right at the surface so that when trouble hits. Bang! We react! Armed with all we think we know we stand ready to make a difference, to fix the problem and to make it safe. We are ready to save those we love. No need for a cape or mask, we stand hands on our hips ready to save the day.

We walk a fine line between surrendering to our God and protecting our loved ones. We hold tightly to our granite-strength-God trusting in Him completely. We hold tighter to all of those we love. Yet, in an instant, it can all change. We fight against the truth that life can change in a split second. We meddle in the lives of love ones trying so hard to keep everyone safe and happy. Letting go is the first step toward freedom. The enemy of Standing on Your Knees living out A Faith Worth Having, the ugly truth, is we **trust** in our own abilities and our small, safe world. Control, trying to control our life is the ugly truth that holds us back from A Faith Worth Having.

Our Facebook, Instrgram, Pinterest life, what I call the air brushed version of our life, reveals only those things we desire to share and show off. We create our own personalized highlight reel. While controlling and creating outward virtual beauty, our real life has a mystery odor. Our insides are rotting away. Catching a whiff from our little corner of the universe it is obvious something stinks! Ignoring the call to bring our brokenness to our supernatural Healer, our Redeemer and our Restorer, we ask for God's blessings, yet we limit Him in what he is allowed to do. We want safe. We want to control our life. We want a God who is safe, understandable, routine, predictable and logical. God is many things. Safe, routine, predictable and logical are not on His profile page. Life is Hard is not a product of immaturity. These are the challenges of those who have walked faithfully with God for years. Gone is the promise that my life is just one wonderful adventure after another.

The enemy of A Faith Worth Having in one word is **control**. The remedy of control is letting go. Releasing everything is not a "pretend life is wonderful, fake smile, never authentically share, always act as if everything is okay, hiding the hideous truth" cure. Authentic letting go knows life can crash and tough things can slam into our loved ones. Everything can fall apart in an instant. In the midst of these tough challenging circumstances we do not call out to a super hero, genie, make my wish come true god. No, we can cry out to the amazing, indescribable, wild, unpredictably loving, warm, always near, steadfast God of the universe. We can live knowing whatever happens the end of our story is a happy ending. We can look forward to a paradise-forever existence with fellow followers of Jesus those from our earthly family and our adopted-lovers-of-Jesus family. Our foolish attempt to control our story is like trying to rewrite the ending of a novel after only reading to the middle of a book. How many editors would stop reading halfway through a manuscript and begin to altar the plot completely believing he knew best? Clueless the editor would have no idea of the story's plot, twists and turns. That's us. So often we want to decide what happens next. We want to take over in the middle. We believe we simply know what is best without any knowledge of the plot or character development and without the understanding of our beautiful ending, our beautifully-broken ending. Clueless, we are about to ruin our own story.

We need to first accept the ugly truth life is not safe and we are not in control. We don't own this life. Longevity is not the goal of our three hundred and sixty-five days we joyously mark with cake, ice cream and presents. We claim each year as our right-our destiny. We just get to hold this life for a little while. There are no guarantees. We live like kings and queens reigning over our hamlet, but we are truly emperors and empresses without any clothes. If we let go and accept the truth, the only thing we control is our response to the hard. If we seek out our evergreen-forever-near God, we are at the beginning of something life altering. We are standing at the cusp of moving from mature to complete. We on the edge of moving toward Standing on our Knees Living out a Faith Worth Having.

Let go, release and free fall into these words.

Fall into His wild, unpredictable, untamed arms. Fall into the everlasting arms that never fail. Stand on His unsinkable, stable and constant ground. Run into a broken world knowing you hold the remedy. Risk it all. Receive what only the here yesterday, here today and here tomorrow God gives. Release all control giving everything over to the ocean maker, mountain creator, sky whisper, DNA designer, forest builder, wild flower producer, star generator, rainbow constructor, infant adopter, love author, grace composer and peace builder. Drive into love that never quits. Hurry toward the One who holds everything leaving you free to explore and enjoy all He has provided. Pour out into Him who carries it all. Gush toward the truth that lives in The One. Flood the world with His grace and love. Throw to others the only hope, the way, the only lifeline, Jesus. Let His peace spill over into everything and everyone you meet. Rush to meet the One whose love never disappoints, never fails and never quits. Hold onto Him and He will hold onto you. Throughout eternity His forever hands hold tight.

Amen

CHAPTER 7

Trust or Crack

The truth is we don't know what we are doing. We want to live a fruitful and happy life. Take off the mask. Take off the best version of the self we want the world to see. Admit the truth. We have no idea what we are doing! We can try to create a small, safe circle traveling through life never risking much and attempting to avoid almost all disappointment. Unfortunately, we can't make life safe, but we can make life small. We can choose to live small.

The Navy Seals do what is called *life altering* training. People in life altering training are thrust into situations in which they either trust or crack.

Trust-staying in while pushing their mind and their body to the very limit, the absolute edge
Crack-give up, walk away, quit

The Navy Seals train for hours in the middle of the night up to their shoulders in the frigid, relentless ocean waves. Just a few yards away up on the dry sandy beach, there is fixed on top of a wooden post a bell. A simple bell, and if you ring that bell you can get out of the bone-chilling ocean. You are ushered into a heated shelter, served a hot beverage and wrapped up in warm blankets. You are safe from the struggle, but the ringing of that bell does something else. Ringing that bell states your struggle is over-really over. That bell says you are finished. And that bell tells everyone still struggling, still persevering in the frigid water, someone else caved. Someone couldn't handle the pain. They couldn't handle the unrelenting challenge. They couldn't fight anymore. They couldn't make it as a Navy seal. They quit.

How often have we rung the bell on the beach and said, "I quit. This is too hard. This is not what I signed up for." We ring that bell and say I refuse to trust you God. We silently retreat and give up. We try and fix our problems, our family and our own friends. In frustration because of the difficulty, in arrogance because we truly know so little and in pure defiance because we want our own way, we put our earthly foot down in an angry little stomp! Like the moth drawn to the flame, we in our own feeble strength and limited brain power foolishly attempt to take over. We secretly believe we know better than the God of caterpillars, the Grand Canyon and a million snowflakes. We arrogantly say, "I got this God… no worries, Immutable Father of the Universe… I have figured out the answer." Once again like a two dimensional super hero un-concealing our cape we say, "Out of the way ear maker, forest builder and desert keeper. It is I created from the dirt. I am here to save the day…Um..quick question??? Will you be serving lunch after I save the world….forgot to eat breakfast!" It would be funny if this weren't so true! Trust is worked out on the battle field of life. Life is hard is the threshold we must walk through to begin our journey of Standing on Your Knees living out A Faith Worth Having. Without trust, we cannot move from mature to complete. We have to answer life's call when God asks, "Will you trust Me? Terrifying as it is to peer into the darkness, trust begins when we are willing to go into the unknown. Never trusting is like buying an incredibly powerful sports car, driving it home and parking it **forever.** Living safe not brave is like buying a stunningly, beautiful necklace never wearing it once and placing it in a vault **forever**.

Is trusting easy? If we are totally honest, our answer is "no." Moving away from self-centered toward trusting begins with disciplining our responses and desires from getting our own way toward following God's way. Sounds as simple as just eat less and exercise more. It is simple, yet is also very difficult to achieve. It is a lie to believe growing, changing and moving toward God will be effortless. We have our self-motivated years to unwind. Like standing up to our neck in frigid ocean waves, we have years of doing things our own way to loosen, to unravel and to unlearn. Those first attempts may unleash our deepest frustrations. We may lash out or become completely unhinged! We may retreat, run and hide from this new reality we are facing. The most difficult trust is to hold on to the unseen while all we can see is falling apart. Trusting is not for the faint of heart.

Is there some a route, a road or a secret path we need to find? It is almost too simple to simply trust. Sometimes our mandates from Christian leaders and authors can feel squishy. Here is an example "always be happy in the Lord." How does that work? How does "happy-slap-a-smile-on-it and pretend it doesn't hurt" draw people to Jesus? There is so much more. We need to be willing to risk everything training ourselves to trust. New ways of thinking and responding will be required. Old ways are useless. Effort to change is needed. Only the new will do. Old patterns are hard to break. We thought were right the entire time. Another warning, God wants these truths to be experiential not just academic. He desires we have an experience with them not just read a devotional about them. He desires we walk them not just talk them. He does ask we relinquish our control. He asks us to look to Him and to give over all our perceived rights. He desires we are open allowing Him take us in wherever direction He chooses. Can we lay down our performances, our effort to try and please God? Release our grip on following a set of rules? Rethink the picture we created that equals spiritual maturity? Can we simply trust God is good? Can we simply trust that this Good God loves us and that He loves us no matter our circumstances? Everything we have learned about God moves us toward this truth. God is good. Trusting is not easy. This will not come naturally. Letting go of our control will not be easy. Trusting our God is actually God and working in every circumstance will be the ultimate challenge.

Trust grows when planted in the foundational fixed truth God loves us. I have struggled at times to believe this truth. I have created my own reasons for God's love. I have believed God only loved me "because." I have wasted a lot of time looking for God's affection in my "because." Looking toward my future I thought, God will love me "because" I am a Mom. Then, I thought, God will love me "because" I am serving in a full-time Christian ministry or "because" I have an amazing, impactful career. My "because" became my understanding of my value in and to God. God will only love me "because." Finish your own "because" sentence. God loves me "because" I…then fill in a reason for God's love. Now, take away the "I" and your reason. Insert the word **just**. *God loves me **just** because!* Seeing God's unconditional love can change our trajectory and free us up to trust in the areas where fear has held us back. We are no longer trying to please God. He loves us unconditionally. God gave His son, Jesus, to take our punishment. He is willing to become our substitute taking our consequences for where we have messed up. We no longer need to try and make ourselves worthy of His titanic love. We are free to respond to life through the vantage point of love. When faced with our own Life is Hard moments, hard hours and yes, hard years, we have a true north to follow. We have a good God who loves us just because. Mind-blowing! God first loved us!

Decked out in love, we take our performance off the table. Focusing on God's love as we face those demanding, grueling, jagged hardships, they can transform us. We still have our part to play listening for His gentle voice to lead us through our barely lit cavernous valleys. We still need to look at our actions to ensure this trial is not a direct result of our poor choices. If we are open to His whisper and sure we are not traveling down an ill advised path, then our Life is Hard moments can transform us. We believe, we trust and we cling to the truth God is good. We are now ripe for transformation. Taking performance off the table isn't new. There is a warning for all of us all found in the book of Romans the twelfth chapter. (Romans 12: 1-2) "So here's what I want you to do, God helping you: Take your everyday, ordinary life—your sleeping, eating, going-to-work, and walking-around life—and place it before God as an offering. Embracing what God does for you is the best thing you can do for him."

Change occurs when we stop using our talents, plans, projects and gifts to win favor from God. Simply laying them down, placing our everyday offerings and trusting our tremendously great and powerful God involves everything. We are all in or off on our own. We can either trust or crack. We can put on the truth that God is Good, and He is loving no matter our situation or circumstances, no matter our trials, no matter our celebrations, our blessings, our melt downs or freak outs. He is amazing, spectacular, overflowing, as close as our heart beat, awe inspiring, joy beyond joy, a love that's higher, wider, deeper, closer than we imagine, Holy and wholly other, beyond our comprehension good. We can trust this amazingly good God. He is love. He is good.

May these words shower you with refreshment.

Trust Him, His way, His people and His word no matter our circumstances, no matter the trial, no matter the hardship and no matter the brokenness. Go back to the foundational truth God loves us. Go back to that simple truth which fills volumes of books, hours of sermons and years of devotionals. God is Good. Hold on to trust and keep our bearings. Remember, A Faith Worth Having is executed in joy with complete abandon through worship and by continuously seeking Him in prayer. Live in utter dependence, marked by absolute trust with actions soaked in love, dripping with compassion and allowing us to be at our best when life is at its worst. Follow the One who blazed our trail, created the path and smoothed every road. Go after the One who straightened the curves avoiding the pitfalls, built the bridges and conquered the mountains. Pursue the One who traveled the dark and dusty routes to the place called somewhere wonderful. Celebrate because now all are welcome and all are cherished. Move toward the light that never fails. Watch for the dawn that lifts the night, defeats the shadows and chases away the thick darkness. We stand in our weakness. We trust in His love. We run to rest. Then, we rest in His amazing peace. We push our mind and our body to the very limit, the absolute edge. We trust in our forever present, never far, as near as each breath, good God.

Amen

CHAPTER 8

As Soon As

Even with the words "trust no matter the circumstances because God loves us" still ringing in our ears, many of us will look for an out. Is the Life is Hard journey for the mature? Is there some short cut or special route to safety for a mature believer? Can we, due to our years spent following and pursuing God, bypass the bone-crushing, heart wrenching, bewildering, kick in the teeth, stomach-punched, black hole, complete despair hard? Does our cosmic bargain have any value? Can we avoid the brokenness that this world hands out?

The mature believer doesn't have some special code to avoid the hard stuff. There is no secret handshake to ward off the difficult. In reality if we pay attention while reading scripture, we will notice a seemly backward pattern connected to the phrase "as soon as." We will read when the mature take God driven risks, big faith challenges rather than their life becoming easier, often it becomes more difficult. From the first book in the Bible called Genesis, God tells Abram (the Father of the Jews) to leave his father's house, his country and head out for a land that God will show him. (Gen. 12:1) This is the definition of a big ask. Abram obeys. We would expect God's blessing on this big faith move. What came after his giant-faith-leap? Just nine verses later we read "a famine came to the land." Not what I was expecting when I read this story the first time. *As soon as* Abram leaves his homeland and he enters the promise land-a famine hits. Abram's journey isn't the only story that reveals this seemingly backward truth.

As soon as Moses frees God's people they experience famine. Thousands of former slave babies, toddlers, children, teenagers, parents, grandmas, and grandpas experience a famine, days without water, not hours but days without water. This must have been horrific especially for the most vulnerable. *As soon as* Elijah defeats the false god Baal in front of everyone his life implodes due to a death threat from Queen Jezebel. Elijah is running for his life depressed and exhausted. *As soon as* Jeremiah preaches a God-given message to the Israelites (God's people)

Jeremiah is whipped and put into stocks on display for all to see. *As soon as* David is placed in charge of God's military King Saul, Israel's very first King, attempts to kill David. Even after David had heroically killed the undefeatable giant Goliath, he was now on the run for his life. He was being hunted by his surrogate father the King.

If our goal is happiness, then we spend our treasure and time working toward comfort, stability and worldly joy. We work to create a spiritual bubble or holy cocoon, but this is not the way the inside out, upside down kingdom works. Life is hard and God's goal for us is so much more than just our happiness. God's goal for each of us is that live without a net. Without fear, we live each day joyfully excited and robustly ready to make a difference. Ready to be all in. Ready to surrender it all on the road to possessing A Faith Worth Having. Ready to be at our best when life is at its worst! These *as soon as* situations came directly after obeying a specific call from God or a God driven ask. These *as soon as* moments did not come from a generic everybody-do-better ask, but they came from a personal leap-of-faith direct ask from God. Also, remember not all of our faith challenges are going to be big. Some are going to be a heavy lift of a small burden. Some *as soon as* challenges come after a response by faith to the mundane, the small and the daily grind of everyday life. Crushing blows can happen to the mature in the midst of their obedience. *As soon as* they take a risk to obey, Life is Hard crashes into them.

Have you ever had the privilege of digging a ditch? I have. It was *"super"* fun. Have you ever heard the theory "Faithfully dig a ditch. Dig day after day, then trust God to bring the rain that yields a harvest"? Have you ever had to dig? Dig day after day. We crack the top soil and begin digging-our weekend caring for our mom who cannot remember our name. We stab the shovel into the ground-the finish of another frustrating day with anger co-workers. Hunched over we lift out shovel after shovel full of dirt-the drive three hours to commute to a job making half of what we made last year. Sweat dripping into our eyes mustering our strength, we toss each pile of dirt to the side-the pain of infertility as a family waits to be born. Plunging the shovel in again, and again, and again we continue and with each shovel load we move a heavy lift of a small burden. Straining using muscles we didn't even know we had, this small burden wears on us. It continually pushes us to the edge. Then, after weeks of the same mind numbing effort, looking forward to the answer or the victory, rather than a reprieve or reward we face our *as soon as* challenge. We face just another giant, impenetrable obstacle. Ugh! These hard moments come after simply stepping into a ditch and beginning the monotonous painful chore of digging. Victory is simply hanging in there when everyone else has given up.

Have we confused being faithful with being happy? Do we believe we should put on a grin and battle silently? Where do we give voice to our melt downs? Where do we acknowledge the mature believer's flip out? When a mature hero of the faith goes through the tough times, do we compassionately encourage them to preserver in Jesus while allowing them the space to fall apart? Praying against all odds, loving and comforting as tears flow down another's cheeks, do we weep with those who weep? Where do we celebrate and embrace the life is hard moments, the life is hard days, the hard months and unfortunately, even the hard decades? Caution. It is a delicate balance to grieve with those who grieve and to be empathic with those whose lives are in ruins. It takes a sensitive approach to be a champion for those seemly all alone walking unguarded out into the thrashing waves and drawn into deepest, darkest waters. It is important to just sit with those who are facing impossible circumstances. Trust is always active. That action may be sitting and weeping with those who are walking the pain filled path. Real trust lives within a heart that aches and inside a soul that weeps.

When the trial is finally over, no matter the outcome, we need to choose celebration. We must choose thanksgiving. We rejoice in His provision bowing to the One and Only. We thankfully sing out His praises. We return to the truth that God is good no matter the outcome and no matter the answer. Even if that answer leaves us feeling cheated, ignored and frustrated, we look to our true north toward the heavens to the original and the conceiver of all we hold dear. What if the normal response to life crashing into you and to me was a complete meltdown? What if we didn't worry about outward appearances? What if we didn't feel the need to stand strong? What if we didn't fear our meltdown was going to somehow discourage other believers? Can we let go of the worry and the false belief that we will disappoint God because we crumbled?

Being vulnerable when we are at our worst reflects our trust. Being completely bare reveals how comfortable we feel with those we love. We do not need to pretend with our God or with those who love Him. God is near our brokenness. During a crisis, our flip out reveals an authentic relationship with the daylight maker who hides a plethora of vibrant colors in shimmering shafts of golden sunlight. If our performance, disappointing God and letting down our fellow Christ followers are off the table, then and only then, can we grieve openly. Our faith, our choices, our sacrifices and even our ridiculous weakness have value. In reality, we shy away from collapsing in front of others. A normal freak-out to a heart-wrenching challenge rings true to anyone watching us. A believer's meltdown can point others to the star flinging fingers, the planet constructor, the designer of the Milky Way, our One and Only, creator of endless space the Almighty God and our forever love, Jesus.

I believed that my pursuit of God would be rewarded. I wanted to follow three clear points or three clear directives to acquire A Faith Worth Having. Full disclosure, I want to avoid **all** *as soon as* moments. All of them! Faith does not follow our plan. Faith, A Faith Worth Having, begins to grow as we come to the end of ourselves. Faith explodes when we trust even though it looks impossible. If the impossible is involved, then is faith just amazing courage? Is faith similar to the amazing courage it takes to walk across a tight rope? I spent some time trying to understand and decide if I agreed with this analogy.

To figure out how I felt, I pictured myself walking across a tight rope. Getting ready to walk out on a thin cable stretched across two imposing sky-scrappers, I stood breathless. One foot inched toward the rope with the wind pushing against me. Terrified, I attempted to find my footing. Swallowing hard, I took several deep breaths. I stepped out onto that high wire. This act, stepping out onto the high wire, is not an accurate picture of A Faith Worth Having. Let's move on. As I cautiously moved out and away from the edge of the building, I saw the giant spans of empty space below. Edging out a little more and using my core strength to maintain my balance, I took small careful steps. Eventually, I edged out to the middle-the place of no return. Inching out barely moving, picture that death defying act balancing on a wire risking everything the wind howling, my toes gripping, this isn't a true illustration of A Faith Worth Having either. At the place of no return, some might say I was living A Faith Worth Having. It does takes courage to walk out to the middle of a tight rope, but standing in the middle ten stories up isn't a true picture of A Faith Worth Having. Stay with me up on that tight rope. Imagine now after several courage-filled steps out of nowhere a wallop of wind knocked me off my balance. I shifted my weight. Remembering my training, focusing using all of my skill and courage, I attempted to regain my footing. Even this horrifying, anxiety-filled moment marked by herculean effort and intense focus isn't a real portrait of A Faith Worth Having.

The wind thrashed again. This time I couldn't recover. Falling, falling faster, falling down toward the concrete, my body began to pick up speed, and I began to brace for it. No net. Soaring toward the pavement, an impossible circumstance, nothing to grab onto, falling faster, zero power, facing tragedy in the making, falling, no plans of escape, falling I have entered the sweet spot. Finally, I am on my way to A Faith Worth Having. When life crashes into us, it is a freefall. We fall faster and faster. When we let go and we trust against the impossible, we are on our way. We are beginning to experience the genuine faith that allows us to be at our best when life is at its worst.

As soon as trials can come at us like a burst of wind from nowhere. They knock us into a freefall. In the midst of obedience, we may be ridiculed, hurt or forgotten. We experience depression, overwhelming stress or debilitating panic. We suffer abuse and may even be stabbed in the back. After our obedience-in-action step of faith, the next thing we face might be the destruction of our dreams, the ruin of our plans or the worst, grim news for our loved one. God does not promise us some equation where faith choices equal success, desired outcomes and relief. He promises it will be hard. He promises His presence. He promises He will hold on to us. And, He promises ultimate victory. Psalm 46:1-3 "God is a safe place to hide, ready to help when we need Him. We stand fearless at the cliff-edge of doom, courageous in sea storm and earthquake, before the rush and roar of oceans, tremors that shift mountains. Jacob-wrestling God fights for us, God-of-Angel-Armies protects us."

True faith, A Faith Worth Having, lives and breathes not just in a leap into the unknown, but true faith explodes in the terrifying freefall. Trusting in mid air with no solution in sight while plummeting toward disaster, A Faith Worth Having takes root. When our plans, our ideas and our control mean nothing, when life is at its worst or when we are falling toward an imminent crash, our faith is the most palpable and the most authentic. Can we trust during these impossible circumstances? If our body is broken do we have the faith God will heal us? If healing isn't a part of our story, do we have the faith God will sustain us and deliver us during the journey to our new normal living in chronic pain?

A young mother faced her *as soon as* moment early one spring day. Infertility had become their new normal. Blessed with two beautiful children, they believed God desired to grow their family. They began the arduous task of qualifying for foster care. Redoing their guest room into a kid friendly space able to accommodate two kiddos, they worked to create a safe landing for a little one in need. She put her shopping skills to good use buying two cribs, several sheets, diapers, those cute towels with hood to cover a baby's sweet little noggin, pink sippy cups and blue sippy cups, lots of clothes and of course a bunch of toys. Even with the latest haul sorted and put away, her list went on and on. They needed to have enough basics to wrap their love around a girl or a boy ages infant to preschooler. Then, God's blessing. We are pregnant! Believing God was affirming their obedience, they wondered would the doctor discover a double blessing? Did they dare to believe the nursery was set up for twins? Off to a routine appointment, her girlfriends waited excited to hear the good news. Then, her *as soon as* moment came. Gut-wrenching. Heart-racking. No heart beat. Why? Why now?

No reason other than Life is Hard works in these desperately sad moments. God is Good. I have seen this mother and father in action. They weathered this storm with beauty and grace. I witnessed their hearts chasing after God. I believe this family will grow. God is Good. Each life matters. God is Good and Heaven is Sure. Our equation faith equals blessing needs to be seasoned with the truth that *as soon as* moments can follow the biggest God driven risks we take. Our trust becomes concrete inside the completely unknown. In the impossible circumstances where there are no easy answers, we live out A Faith Worth Having. It almost doesn't feel like faith. We have so little to give. Here is where our faith is redefined, refined and then gently explodes impacting a dying and broken world. Here is where we are transformed. Here is where we learn to be at our best when life is at its worst. Desperately falling through impossible circumstances, here is where we live out A Faith Worth Having.

Feel His warmth wrap around you

Trust His presence. Hear His joy bursting through with answers brimming with healing. Live and love showered in blessings of friendship and family. Never worry God's never-late, never-early surprises are just beyond "I can't take this a minute longer!" The sovereign One is there, right there where it hurts and right there where it is unbearable. He is near in the confusing when grief is crushing. We weep reaching toward Him our hearts long for Him. We sing out because speech feels inadequate. Drink in the everlasting indescribable moments. Look to the horizon and see the forever kingdom starting now. Follow the sacred One, the One who gave His everything, so we could have anything. Feel His warmth wrapping tight around us lighting the narrow way. Rush toward His presence a refuge and a stronghold. He is a comfy cozy couch. We wait knowing His best is near maybe today or maybe tomorrow. Secure we now wait. We wait in Him. There it is in the waiting, while waiting trust blooms. Trust in the One who knows our name, sees our heart and holds our soul. Life is hard, the cross. God is good, Jesus. Heaven is Sure, our forever life with our forever family awaits. Our forever Heaven is Sure. Trust, trusting in the One who never fails is the beginning, the entrance and first step toward life-impacting-faith.

Amen

CHAPTER 9

Living Palms Up

We don't go looking for impossible situations that require complete trust or A Faith Worth Having. We want life to be predictable and easy, if not easy, then at least easier. We believe that we can work to increase our faith. Put in time and energy and out pops grown-up faith. We want to be able to assess the risk, calculate several contingency plans, brace ourselves, then and only then, we will step into the unknown. We fool ourselves believing God works according to our desires as we take our faith steps. We need to unshackle our minds and hearts from our preconceived outcomes. We need to be active as we respond to this often dismal, gloomy, broken Life is Hard world

If you have experienced contemporary worship you have probably seen someone raise their hands during the music and singing? What if this gesture I'll call "palms up" became a concrete, active response to God? What if palms up began the conversation with our One and Only, the Almighty? What if palms up or the raising our hands was letting go? What if palms up meant we are throwing our pain toward Him. What if palms up indicated we are opening our hands to release our frustrations and our anxieties while reconfirming our trust in God. And then finally, what if palms up meant we are ready to travel with Him wherever He leads. In humility our walls fall down and our tender hearts open as we reach out to Him, our God-intimacy is deepening. Living palms up, we become ordinary angels with A Faith Worth Having giving out the practical help others need. Living palms up is not just as a catch phrase, a Christian slogan or a nice sentiment. Living palms up is choosing to live in a distinct way. Living palms up is standing open before God risking all without a net, and the outcome may be a terrifying freefall.

Nothing is more clarifying than scarcity, hardship and brokenness. The unspoken truth we don't want to hear is God allows us to suffer extreme needs. Attempting to deflect the pain from the hardship, we complain. We can become discouraged. We can feel like quitting. These hardships and brokenness can reveal our true nature. Equally terrifying as "nothing is more clarifying than scarcity, hardship and brokenness" is the statement, "Growth begins after our hardships or our battles moving us deeper into God's story." These battles, overwhelmingly big or irritatingly little, they are physical, emotional, spiritual, material and relational. These battles are everywhere.

Have you and I ever been driven, not "Hey, I think I will try to spend some time with God if I can find it," but driven into His Presence? Have we ever been desperate for His comfort, reassurance and guidance? God has been allowing hardships then answering in purposeful unconventional means from the beginning. After hundreds of years in captivity with forty extra years of wilderness wondering following a rebellion after the "jumped out of the fire" golden calf incident, I thought those who finally made it into the Promise Land deserved a little vacation. A trip to a beach, perhaps? A spa treatment? They had paid their dues and then some. What was next for God's chosen people, the nation called Israel, after four hundred years living as slaves in a foreign land? Vaca? A Spa day? A few weeks at the beach? Nope, what came next were battles, hardships and more battles. The Israelite's reward for surviving horrific circumstances, deeply unfair practices and life threatening challenges was a battle with more battles to come. Why didn't God just get rid of all of the nations who threatened Israel's existence? Why didn't God just wipe out the Amorites, Hittites, Edomites, Canaanites and the menacing Badguyites? Why did Israel have to fight? Why all the battles?? During these battles for the Promised Land the Israelites had to trust completely. God changed His methods for achieving victory. They couldn't create a victory game plan and follow it. They were asked to lay down their preconceived, self-infused ideas and trust God daily. Their very lives depended on absolutely resting in a unpredictable, inexplicable, surprising God.

Trust is exercised when a sacrifice or a loss is a distinct possibility. Trust is deep and real when we are forced to choose between two extremely different options. Trust grows when we can lose something we value. Trust deepens when choosing God's way could mean greater hardship or greater difficulty. Trust is born in the belly of demanding choices. Trust is strengthened when our free will is tested. Trust ignites when the unknown is weathered. When asked to risk it all, choosing to trust becomes the believer's ultimate proving ground. How do we know that we are choosing to follow God? Are we just following other Christians? How do we know if we are living palms up or tightly clutching all we have? How do we measure whether we are risking it all or playing it safe?

Lindsey woke up and read these words in her daily devotional. "Trust Me no matter the difficulty or challenge today. Trust me and you will feel satisfied!" "Great!," thought Lindsey. Later that afternoon, she found herself getting extremely hungry. Unfortunately, the only restaurant for miles had only two choices left on the menu. And, Lindsey was not the only hungry patron waiting for a satisfying meal. Lindsey over hear the conversation from the next table. Due to some crazy circumstances, the woman sitting next to Lindsey has not eaten in two days. Was this going to be a chance to live out her Christian conviction of putting others first? Then, the only two choices appeared. A cheeseburger or wait for it….a bacon cheeseburger! Yummy! Vegetarians enter your favorite veggie burgers above. Lindsey loved cheeseburgers and knew after this meal she would feel satisfied. She praised God thanking Him for His provisions. There wasn't much risk or difficulty in trusting God's provision when the choices were cheeseburger or bacon cheeseburger. No real difference and no cost. Now the situation is the same but the choices are left different. The two choices on menu are a cheeseburger or a raw kale salad and seven carrot sticks??? Lindsey was not a big fan of kale. She let the other woman order first. She ordered a cheeseburger. Say goodbye to that juicy cheeseburger, Lindsey!?! Now can she trust that God will satisfy her? This "lunchtime conundrum" illustrates that our level of commitment hides inside the difficulty and complexity of our choices. Likewise, if our choices are always easy or equal, then we are not risking or trusting at all.

Our free will is put to the test when our choice costs us something. Our free will is tested when we can lose. Our free will is tested when life crashes into us and we lose everything we hold dear. Can we trust when we experience a grueling, challenging ordeal? Bottom line, can we trust when our choice is to live palms up and to follow God costing us everything? The deeper, the harder the choice we face the more we can grow. Our trusting sacrifice strengthens our souls and moves us toward exercising our faith. We move from mature to complete by wrestling with very difficult choices. If the choices we face are always easy, they will cost us very little, and we will never grow to trust. We will never live palms up.

One of the hardest choices is to trust God in an impossible circumstance. We desire to control, to fix, to change and to repair. We believe we know better than the creator of the Milky Way. We believe we can do better than the Always Almighty. We are the clay crying out to the potter, "Mold me this way! Definitely not that way!" Even the fathers of our faith had choices that tugged at their resolve and pulled at their trust in God. David was hiding in a cave when his enemy, the person who had made his life horrible, enters. David must have felt overwhelmed. This enemy was unaware and completely vulnerable. David's choice was to eliminate the guy who had him running for his life or to obey God letting his enemy, the anointed King, go. Should David respect the anointed one or should he give into his revenge-ready hands? David's enemy was a fellow believer Israel's first king. He had been David's mentor just a few months earlier, but now he had betrayed David and hunted him like a dog. David could make the case he had every right to fight back, to end the madness and to conquer an out of control enemy. In his trust or crack moment, David chose to obey God sparing King Saul. Trust or Crack. Live Palms Up.

A prophet named Elijah, who had defended God during dark oppressive times, received his call to trust after his amazing obedience lead to a terrifying choice. After defeating the prophets of Baal and revealing Israel's heresy of worshipping false gods, Elijah's very life was threatened. What would Elijah, a seasoned follower of God, do? Face death or in object failure run in fear? After taking a monumental stand in faith for God, Elijah ran. He ran and ran and ran. Exhausted he collapsed, and he was done. Life seemed completely unbearable. Paralyzed by overwhelming fear, he cried out to die. On his own, far away from the crowds, Elijah slowly changed course. He chose to accept God's comforts. He snacked on fresh baked bread as the aroma surrounded him like a warm blanket on a chilly night. Then, after a perfectly timed nap, Elijah stood ready. Elijah received a personal sermon from the ultimate communicator God Himself. Elijah lived out the rest of his life with A Faith Worth Having. At the end of his life a fiery chariot, the original hotrod, took him to see his God face to face. Trust or Crack. Live Palms Up.

Our choices will look different, but ultimately they are all about trusting God. Be warned, we will all have our own *as soon as* moments. Accept the fact that even spiritual heroes, faith giants will be tested big time. When our impossible choice comes, when faced with our challenge, when life crashes into us, let our response be the essence of following Jesus. Let our choice be to trust the one who hides thunder in clouds. It sounds so simple, simply choose to trust. But, those of us who have walked this path know how difficult it is to trust in this shattered, cruel, unfair world. In spite of the impossible that appears impenetrable choose to live palms up. Trust don't crack.

Don't be fooled by the cereal aisle of life the over abundance of our choices. There are just two choices in this life. We choose to trust or we choose to crack. Choose to trust. We can choose to live palms up throwing our pain toward God. We can open our hands releasing our frustration and our anxiety. We can reconfirm our trust in God. Follow God wherever He leads. When our walls are down and our hearts open, we reach out to God and our intimacy with Him deepens. No matter the circumstances we can live palms up. We **can** become ordinary angels with A Faith Worth Having giving out the practical help others need. Life offers two choices trust or crack. Life offers two ways to live fists clenched or palms up. When life is hard, choose to trust. Choose to live palms up.

Resting in His ways run into His arms

Make a run for God-we won't regret it. Stop fighting a fight that's already been won. Forget regret and defeat. The Earth-tamer, Ocean-pourer, Mountain-maker, Hill-dresser, Sea storm and Wave Muzzler will be the solid rock under our feet. He will be the breathing room for our soul. Wake up. It is our "when at last" and "suddenly spring" moment. Amazing life altering outcomes are real. Be secure in His presence knowing His dependable love shows up on time releasing us from earth bound thoughts. Stand in awe of God's yes, banking His promises in the vault of our heart. Remember all our springs are in Him. Walk through the rose petals, the wild meadows and the green grass that carpets the earth glistening under sweet rain. Rest in Jesus. He is our granite strength, our safe harbor and our ever present. We raise our arms as a praise banner. Skip, run and play. We hold onto Him for dear Life. Trust Him, the I Am, the Messiah, riding a train of hallelujahs. In His arms, we'll find safety. Heaped with goodness-in-action His arms reach out. Tell the next generation detail by detail the Forever-God story. Tell all. He set these once broken bones dancing. Dancing down the desperate, dingy roads on earth, we'll travel onto the magnificent, shining streets of gold, woven though out glory. Choose to live palms up and choose to trust Him. Fall into forever arms forever covered by a forever love.

Amen

CHAPTER 10

White Sand, Plain Listening, and Rest

In pursuit of deeper faith, I set up my cosmic bargain. I did my best for Him. I gave God more of my life, my wants and my wishes. I never said it out loud, but I believed as I matured and gave more to God, then He was bound by some oath to protect me and to bless me. But, I couldn't seem to find my footing. I was desperately trying to follow every rule, every ritual and every routine. I was determined to please God and please everyone else. God's story and Jesus life refuted my desire to make my life always equal, always happy and never disappointing. I learned nothing was off limits. Like surviving a severe hurricane, I found faith after much of my life was gone. Life is Hard.

Receive one call and everything changes. Job lost. It's cancer. Death is near. Or a heavy lift of a small burden, those frustrating and incredibly irritating daily parts of life like walking on tiny bits of glass. Daily migraines. Complaining Co-workers. Three hours of third grade homework-every night. Whether it is a blazing-red-hot fire storm or a low grade fever, both are uncomfortable and both work to refine us. The fever or the fire storm work daily to change us, to reform us and to redirect us. I needed to learn there was a threshold I had to walk through to begin my journey toward A Faith Worth Having. That threshold can be a fire storm or a persistent, low grade fever. I had to trust that my Life is Hard moments were the defining moments that would lead me to a life worth living. Trust is only worked out on the battle field of life. I could choose to either live Palms Up or fists clenched. I could choose to either trust or crack.

When we can't seem to find the balance to stand tall, what's the problem? Maybe the answer lies not in our head but in our stance, our feet and where they stand. From Proverbs 12:3 "You can't find firm footing in a swamp, but life rooted in God stands firm." Who would try to take a stand in a swamp!?! One of my favorite preschool Bible story songs was about the importance of strict building codes. "The wise man built his house upon the rock and a foolish man built his house upon the sand." We sang out "The rain came down and the floods came up…the rain came down and the floods came up…the rain came down and the flood came up and foolish man's house went splat!?!" Our hands smacked together as we gleefully shouted "Splat!"

I don't think we ever understood we were celebrating a collapse of someone's house!?! No one chooses to build on a unstable foundation like sand over the firm foundation on solid rock. (Matthew 7:25-27) "If you work these words into your life, you are like a smart carpenter who built his house on solid rock. Rain poured down, the river flooded, a tornado hit—but nothing moved that house. It was fixed to the rock. But if you just use my words in Bible studies and don't work them into your life, you are like a foolish carpenter who built his house on the sandy beach. When a storm rolled in and the waves came up, it collapsed like a house of cards." Splat!

Ever wonder why life is seems so unstable? Ever wonder why we can't build anything that lasts. It all goes "Splat!" Ever wonder if we have become the numb arm of the Christian faith? Maybe our lack of strength comes from spending days unable to get our footing because we are standing in sand, beautiful white sand. I never worried about my foundation. I was too busy marveling at the beautiful white sand beneath my very unsteady feet. What is white sand? White sand is all the good things we worship either instead of God or equal to God. If our health, our family, our ministry or our career is worshipped together with God, then it is white sand. Even those activities we feel make a difference in this broken world can become a white sand trap. The ultimate sandbox, Facebook or Istagram, is where our vacations, our outings, our family photos, our goofy poses and even our ministry efforts are on display. Here is where we share our lives with family and friends. We display our faith, our tributes to God and our challenges to other believers. Is here one day and gone the next, a Facebook way of worshiping our personal wildflowers? Do we put our life experiences on pedestals "Wowing, Ooooing, and Aahhhing" at all we do for God and for each other. It's tempting to be impressed by our rolling newsfeed life. Anything instead of an authentic pursuit of God we use to fuel our souls will leave us stuck in white sand spinning our wheels. If we mistakenly try to get refueled using our good efforts, then our output for the kingdom will be zero. Worshipping what we do for God has no power to transform us. If the only time we engage the Holy One is to bless our plans, our ideas and our way of serving Him, then we are running on fumes. We are building on unpredictable, beautiful, useless, white sand.

We believe busy equals productive. We trust in our white sand contributions. We believe the way to God's heart is through action. This is not what scripture teaches us. Scripture is filled with references of God's people resting. Obviously, there is the original, the Sabbath, a true day of rest from work and effort. In the most dramatic call to rest, God set apart an entire year called the Year of Jubilee. This year gave a rest to the farmland, the slaves and prisoners were given their freedom and all debts were forgiven. I don't think this went over very well with the rich and powerful!?! Even Jesus went off by himself to rest, recharge and reconnect with the Father. The truth is busy equals numb. Busy leads to self-centered control freaks. It is easier and faster if we do it ourselves which leads to exhaustion that dulls our senses and reflexes. Our spiritual interactions suffer right along with the rest our body. God is serious about rest. Those of us who love a two hour nap are grabbing our favorite pillow and looking for a cozy place to crash right now!

When we rest, we can accurately hear from God. After a battle for part of the promise land Saul, Israel's first king, was told **not** to keep the plunder not to keep anything or anyone from the defeated kingdom. Saul disobeys keeping the opposing king alive also keeping some victory tokens. Samuel, God's voice in those pre-holy spirit days, comes along and with the sound of the enemy's prize sheep bleating in his ears says to King Saul, "Do you think all God wants are sacrifices---empty rituals just for show? He wants you to listen to Him. Plain listening is the thing, not staging lavish religious production (white sand). Not doing what God tells you is far worse than fooling around in the Occult. Getting self-important around God is far worse than making deals with dead ancestors. Because you said No to God's command He says No to your Kingship" (1 Samuel 15:22-23) Ignoring God and going our own way begins when we choose not to slow up, not to listen and not to heed God's words. God is serious that we are paying attention and plain listening. When we slow down, we can follow His daily instructions. Not following those instructions is far worse than fooling around with occult. I read this several times. It still catches my breath. God is extremely serious when it comes to our listening. We have the strength to follow Him whole-heartedly. We can see God for who He is and see our self-significance for what it is. Our created self-importance can be the parasite than wrecks us from the inside. God knows how debilitating this way of living can be. He knows the waste we create when we live for ourselves. Our wheels grind to a halt unable to change the world for Him. God knows how being double minded trying to serve two masters, living for God and living for ourselves, is our Achilles' heel. It's our kryptonite creating weakness in everything we do.

Science also speaks to the affects of being over tired. Studies have shown driving sleep deprived is the same as driving under the influence. What about living sleep deprived? Living perpetually fatigued? What kind of life comes out of this state? Over activity and busyness numbs all the senses-spiritual included. Vision becomes blurry. We can see only as far as our next deadline, next goal or next task. Our lives are white sand focused. We are stumbling through life feeling as though something is missing, yet we are too tired to try and figure it out. We are running to nowhere. Like a hamster running inside a metal wheel confused by his lack of progress. He can't seem to stop his little feet from grabbing for the next metal rung. He is spinning himself to nowhere. Always on the go, and never getting anywhere. Our wheel spins on. Ironically, our over-active life blocks our movement forward. We are white sand driven, numb, self-seeking, self-interested, self-focused and struggling from self-centered tunnel vision. We are trying to fix it all balancing an elephant on a toothpick trying to move forward by running in place. If idle hands are the devil's workshop, then over scheduled lives are the devil's vacation days. Sinking deeper and deeper into overwhelming exhaustion, we mess up our lives with each sleep deprived stumble we take.

What limits the Christian church today is so few of us "mature" believers slow down long enough to maintain with any regularity the life altering spiritual practices we crave. We are bombarded in life with things we need to do to get better and to be better. Spend ten minutes watching TV, surfing the net or thumbing through your Facebook newsfeed. Take this class and conquer the world. Wear this suit and be a financial winner. Drive this car and live on the edge. Buy this particular house and have the perfect family. Eat this and lose weight. Live secure, live successful and of course, live happily ever after. On and on it goes we grasp to get ahead and our metal wheel spins again. With every whirl of the wheel, we are told what we need to be healthy, happy and secure. Cinderella ditch that prince, because Facebook, Pinterest and Instagram have figured the one true path to happily ever after!?! Our goal all along has been to have A Faith Worth Having, and we have learned happy and faithful do not always go together. White sand is getting us nowhere fast. So how do we combat our white sand addiction? For those of us who desire five clear points to combat white sand are going to be disappointed. Ready? Stop, a one word answer. Stop.

Stop, then get off the get- it-done-now-burn-out-super-fast-highway. Let go of all the pressure and frustration from trying to find firm footing while standing out in the middle of white sand. Stop and listen to the ear-maker, sunset painter, song bird composer. Stop. Sleep deprived, over scheduled, exhausted, stressed-out crabby warriors do not last very long in the battle, if they even make it to the battle at all. The world is dying faster than we can make disciples, so we don't have the time to waste any time swirling inside a cloud of over-scheduled, never a minute to spare, demanding lives. Stop, rest and regain your footing on that firm foundation the Rock!

Let these words carry you into His presence

Reach for more. Rest in Him. Know we are marked by grace, created for greatness and designed by the ultimate master craftsman. We are a once in a lifetime, superbly gifted, critical part of the kingdom. He made us for great things. Rest in His comforts. We have His truth, His love and His everlasting arms that never fail. Be still and know. Be still and trust. Be still. Just be still. Lovers of His name lay down all that holds us back. Are we running in circles without Him? Are we running nowhere fast? He knows our name. His joy is finding us. Live in the quiet spaces where we can see a shadow of His Face. God made it all and stands joyfully in the gap for you and for me. What a privilege to be with His people, His joy, and His delight. His traits are in His children. See our Father's eyes, His smile, His warmth and His compassion in those who are His dear ones. In His green pastures where we find His protection and a safe haven, rest and lay our weary heads down. Glory waits for those who rest in His never late, His never early and His just at the right time. Praise Him, in adoration and in triumphant, in beauty and in delight, in majestic grandeur and in sumptuous splendor, in pomp and in celebrations, praise Him our glorious One who lives forever and always prevails-the Victor. He is the first and the last, our Savior and our friend, praise Him always. May we rest in the deepest comfort known to man. Resting in the Only One, the perfect One, who took on our fight and gave us the spoils. Justice battles. Mercy wins. Rest in the green meadows at the feet of the greatest shepherd. Rest in Jesus the sweetest name.

Amen

CHAPTER 11

Day by Day, Always Moving and Crying Out

I can still see her sitting on the couch with a cup of tea and her Bible open. This is how she started each day. I wanted to be just like her, so about age twelve I began my day with a teenage devotional, my Bible and a cup of tea. Later I think my cosmic bargain crept in to this deeply personal time with God. I believed my time in God's word, prayer and loving others would bound God to fulfill my wishes. Later, when my life fell apart it was harder to maintain this habit. Working through my heart aches, my mistakes and just the hard that had become my journey, I rediscovered the joy in spending time in Day by Day practices. Lived out in a humble and an expectant manner, the Day by Day practices are authentic conversations with God, searching the scriptures to learn about God and hear from Him personally and living in an "others first community." I didn't realize that beyond connecting us to the Almighty, the natural consequence from these persistent practices is a complete heart revolution.

The engine of A Faith Worth Having is a heart that trusts through any situation. The practice of Standing on Your Knees is strengthened by daily saying yes to God when very little is at stake. I thought trust would grow as I learned more and did more. I never connected my ability to trust with my ability to simply make time for Day by Day practices. It makes perfect sense. If I cannot trust God with twenty minutes of my day or with seventy-five minutes a week to attend weekly worship, then I will never trust Him with my hard times, big hurts and brokenness. I won't trust Him with my life or the fate of my loved ones. There is a direct connection between spending time in God's word, prayer, living life with other-centered believers and A Faith Worth Having.

If we only do Day by Day practices when we feel like it or only when our over-scheduled life allows, then we have discovered our stumbling block. Saying yes to God with very little at stake leads to a responsive heart. Strengthened and primed to be open, throwing our pain and our brokenness toward His heart is the game changer. Saying yes when very little is at stake leads to saying yes when everything we care about is on the table. We can be our best when life is at its worst. Day by Day practices change our hearts so that we have the guts to lay it all on the line.

This Day by Day growth happens behind the scenes. No one but you or I will know the truth. We can put on a good front, talk a good game, saying all the "right" things, even tricking ourselves into justifying our lack of passion. Our lack of growth will limit our impact and hurt those we love. When we live out of our self-centeredness, we hurt everyone around us with our weak responses. We hold back progress, because we are thwarting our own growth. This can happen over a long period of time without a life altering challenge. Without any Day by Day living, our journey can become a stale, splintered life lived out in shattered, small pieces.

We desire a deeper faith. We have a mountain top exciting experience and say "I am changed forever. I will never look back. The old me is gone." What we should say is we have experienced something special and something new. We may look at life a little differently now. We have added this new experience into our life story. True change or real transformation involves a completely new path and a complete turn-around. Day by Day commitments, practices and priorities move us to slow down and steady us in the right direction. Even the smallest amount given can move us toward a transformed, redeemed, rescue story. A heart engaged in Day by Day growth says yes to the little and begins the journey toward saying yes to the big. We can move from living small to living big. We can move from living safe to living brave. We can move toward taking concrete trusting steps. Moving inches or by miles, Day by Day practices give us the momentum that moves us forward and wards off decline. A simple change like daily reading God's word and spending time praying are the green shoots that eventually grow into a garden that bears life altering fruit. When twenty minutes of our day is freely given to the One who created time yet is not bound by time, our faith grows. The life changing payoff is the guts to say yes when **everything** we care about is at stake. God commands us to follow Him daily. Obedience has its own rewards. Our Day by Day practices prepare us for our glorious, magnificent, awe inspiring, jaw-dropping future.

This side of heaven our spiritual life is always in motion. It's always moving. We never stand still. We are growing or retreating. We are growing in our faith and our trust in God, or we are shrinking away and falling backward. Sometimes we fool ourselves into thinking everything is fine. But if we are not growing, then we are in the midst of retreat. We retreat to self comfort, self protective, unproductive and self centered living. We move forward or we fall backward.

Daddies don't disappear overnight. Families don't crumble in a day. Life doesn't go off the rails just because of what happened this morning. We are never stand still. We are always moving toward God or away from God. We are growing closer to God or moving toward our selfish self. We are always moving in the direction we pursue. We travel through the gateway of growth or through an entrance of bleak loss. Our Day by Day growing moves our heart forward even if it is by inches. Every small growth moves us forward. We never stand still. We trust or crack. We live palms up or with clinched fists. We move forward or fall backward.

I love spring. I get excited about the journey from dormant to abundant. I look forward to lush, prolific growth. After a recent bitter, bitter cold winter, when three layers of clothes were not enough and when our bones ached from the wind chill while our teeth chattered, "How soon until this car warms up??? This frigid, snow layered, icy, freezing…Ugh! My scraper just broke winter?!?" That's a description of one weekend in Indiana during the month of January in 2014. Spring could not come fast enough! The colossal beauty we enjoy during this long awaited season comes out slowly. Incremental day by day growth brings out each small change. Most of us probably miss this change, then WHAM! Everything is in bloom! How many of us ever notice those tiny baby leaves on our trees? Do we notice the tired brownish grass transform over night waking up bright green? Who pays attention to those tiny buds appearing out of nowhere bursting forth into spectacular, stunningly beautiful flowers? Each day things are changing. Every day things are growing. Day by Day growing. WHAM! Spring seemingly from nowhere arrives in all its glory! Daily saying yes to God when very little is at stake will lead to a "suddenly spring" moment. When it's all on the line, we'll be able to throw our pain and our brokenness toward God. Saying yes, when very little is on the table, will lead to saying yes when everything we care about lies open, vulnerable and at risk. It can still take our breath away. It will still hurt, deeply hurt. If we have been moving toward God, we'll be better prepared for those heart-wrenching moments when life crashes into us!

As we move toward God, pain will still find us, so when it hurts cry out. Today we can unload on Facebook, Twitter or by texting. We cry out to those we trust and truly care about. We fake happiness with everyone else. Think of the person in our life with whom we feel completely safe, and with whom we can be our worst self. It could be a spouse, friend, family member. We are the most alive and vulnerable with those we deeply care about. What about God? Why not let it all go with Him?? Do we feel that our hurting, grieving and struggling are letting Him down? Do we worry we'll reveal we don't have "enough" faith if we vent to God our true feelings? If we open the flood gates of our true feelings do we worry they will overwhelm us and bury us alive? Are we skeptical while wondering will it do any good to let it all go? It won't change anything, so why bother mucking into those dark feelings. We may prefer the stuff-it-down "Be strong, bury those feelings deep inside. Then, gut it out!" way of responding.

Crying out unburdens our hearts and minds. It brings authenticity to our struggle. All through scripture the mature cry out. Think of a work issue we are trying to solve. Here are our options: complain to a co-worker, to a family member or to friends, Google how to solve the problem, get even, burn with anger putting on a brave face pretending things are "okay" while continuing to churn inside. Our simmering frustration will affect of our performance, our attitudes, our interactions with others and our output. Next, let's try crying out to our boss or as the famous frosty princess sings, "Let it go!" Hold nothing back. A good boss will listen then try and help. In scripture, the mature cry out letting it rip with an authentic, deep "ugly cry." They let it all go. Even Jesus cried out. Crying out un-burdens us, and most importantly, it begins the conversation with our God.

Praying often is great. But, the faith altering question is "Are we crying out?" If we're not crying out, then where do we turn when depressing, disorienting anxiety descends on us producing howling heartache? It is a waste of time to just say, "Be strong. Dig deep. Feel better." We know this doesn't work. Deep in a dark hole, we have to trust in a good God and that He is near. From (Psalm 139:1-6 my version) "I'm never out of your sight (God in our present) You know everything I'm going to say. I look behind me you are there (God present in your past) then up ahead and you're there too (God present in our future) Your reassuring presence Coming and Going." God is in our present. God is in our past. God is in our future.

In this fast food, 140 characters, short cut ridden, "It's been a minute 30 seconds!?! What do you mean my chicken nuggets are not done?" world, everything happens at lightning speed. Time isn't useful, unless it is moving faster than fast! Could it be one of the only places in this whirling, hyper-speed world that we can truly see God is while traveling down the road of grief-the Life is Hard journey. We don't like waiting. We move at a supersonic speed, but God has all the time in the world. When forced to stand completely still, we frantically search to make things happen. Again from the book of Psalms, listen for the nearness of God to those who have traveled the darkest road. (Psalm 34:18) "If your heart is broken, you'll find God right there: If you're kicked in the gut He'll help you catch your breath." He is close enough to help us catch our breath. Bone crushing grief reveals how close God has been to us all along. He is nearer than we think. He is close enough to help us breathe when there isn't any air in our lungs. He is near all the time. It's how we look at our trials that determine whether we grow. Are they something to endure? Are they a lesson to learn? Are they something to move beyond? Are we just trying to get to the other side where life becomes fun again? If life can't go back to being fun, then a little less stressful is our goal. If our life turns out the way we hope, then at the very least we desire easy. Standing washed in His grace, we say, "Yes, I surrender to this God sent from heaven in human form." Finally, we are exactly where God wants us. All we need to do is trust Him enough to do "it". Whatever our "it" is, He can and will do it! The answer may not look exactly like we pictured, but God is faithful. He does answer. He is near.

Trust is built thru years of crying out. In the Old Testament they seemed to name everything, not like the names we use today "Butterfly187" or "surfer dude 2018." Life crashed into Abraham when God asked him to sacrifice his only son. Abraham's life was turned upside down. This God-directed event took several days to complete. Directed by God, Abraham had to get supplies then travel to that remote spot. During the preparation and journey, Abraham had plenty of time to completely freak out! When asked by God to sacrifice his one and only son, Abraham completely trusted God is Good. He trusted a miracle would follow after this unimaginable choice. God seemed to be silent until that final moment. God's answer came at the very edge of Abraham's knife, the edge of his seemly super human obedience, just in the nick of time before the sacrificial knife went in to his one and only son. With the knife held high above his son's body, God's answer came, "Stop." Whether a thundering voice or a whisper, the answer came to Abraham "Stop the sacrifice." If I were in Abraham's sandals, I would have preferred to hear the "stop" the morning before the journey. Even better I would have preferred to hear, "stop" before I packed three donkeys for the trip.

Right after God's suddenly "Stop," Abraham sees a ram caught in a thicket by them. The sacrifice was completed. Now, if I were naming this spot, I would have called it, "Seriously, God, Please, please don't test me like that again! Don't ever wreck my heart like that and never, ever ask so much of me. Don't ever ask for my one and only child. Please, I am begging you God never again!"

Abraham called this place, "The Lord will provide"

He trusted God with his all-his ONLY son. Not only was Isaac his beloved son, but he was also the beginning of God's people named Israel. The promised future, Isaac was a long awaited answer. Isaac was the son to carry on the line creating the people of God, the Jews. I believe Abraham risked all because he trusted God was Good and he knew Heaven was Sure.

Abraham believed he would see his son again no matter how the sacrifice ended. In Abraham's path, of pain, of sacrifice and of redemption, we see all three sides to our foundation. Life is Hard. God is Good. Heaven is Sure. Abraham started his trust or crack journey with God late in his life. He was significantly past middle age. A Faith Worth Having can be ours no matter our age or life experiences. Abraham didn't get there overnight. He had failed, risked, been tested and failed again for years, decades even. Abraham had traveled many, many rough roads and confusing miles before he reached this place. "The Lord will provide." Day by Day Abraham grew incrementally. He became stronger in his faith to the point that in his greatest trial he was truly at his best. His response was no accident. He had let go and trusted God. He followed his God and no matter the circumstances his God was faithful.

Today Google has tons of helps to begin our Day by Day practices. Find a church that learns from scriptures and isn't afraid of the believer's freak out. Discover a community that is "other" centered. Begin a conversation with the God of glass-like glaciers and ice filled mountains. These practices of growing daily and of authentically crying out are absolutely critical to life so that when the Life is Hard moments come we will know without a doubt that our God is Good and beyond any fear or failings that Heaven is Sure. Living Day by Day is like breathing, so "breathe in His Presence and breathe out His praise."

Allow these words to challenge and encourage

Move toward a God shaped life abundantly blessed growing in confidence in the magnificent King. Authentically cry out in the present, relinquishing the past and living with abandonment toward the future. Step on a God-blazed-trail. May our steps be steadied by His ever-close-love. Plant a righteous root. May the buds of our life bloom. Plant joy seeds in the good heart soil. Sing into His presence, God's great and terrible, beautiful and mysterious presence. "Breathing in His grace and breathing out His praise" His joy pumps through our heart and reaches out to others. May our lives ripen as beauty and love chases after us. Enter His never-sorry-you-knocked sanctuary. Live in His all generous love. Soar into His always loyal affection. Follow His forever righteousness and His glow-in-the-dark directions. Feel Eden springs cascading through your fingers and find the true fountain of gracious living flowing from His healing touch. His meteoric love and His astronomic forgiveness reveal His titanic purposes. God rewrites the text of our life. Open our heart to see His affection in His eyes. Applaud for Him and His extravagant, always there, setting-everything-right love. He holds you and me secure in His firm hands while He gently caresses our cares away.

Reach for our before, our now, our forever and our always God.

Amen

CHAPTER 12

The Ultimate Freedom Song

Life would be so different if there were never any challenges, set backs or heart aches. What if the sun shone all the time and there was never a night? What if every dream did come true? What if there was no such thing as an unanswered prayer or as a road less traveled just wish "poof" and every dream came true. Think about that honestly. Our lives would be a mess if we got exactly everything we ever wanted. I have spent time with spoiled children. Nothing sours a sweet innocent child like being showered with attention, never being corrected, never experiencing any challenges, pain or loss and never being pushed to grow.

When I was young, I wish someone had taught me the significance of these three concepts. Life is Hard. God is Good. Heaven is sure. I was told God has a wonderful plan for your life. Cool bring it on! But when my life fell apart, I was looking for someone to blame. I knew it couldn't be God. I did what every mature, Bible literate, raised in the church, Christian does. I blamed myself. When I heard the words "wonderful plan," I interpreted that to mean God wants to fulfill my wishes. He wants to follow **my** plan so that my life would always make me happy. When life became hard, unpleasant and frustrating, I felt **I** must be doing something wrong. I pointed the finger at myself. It has taken me years to unwind these false beliefs. If we are honest about our goal for this life, it is to be healthy and happy. Our definition of happy usually means we get exactly what we want. Happiness, our happiness and the happiness of those we love, is our number one priority. We obey God with our time, our treasure and our talents. In return for our obedience, all we want from God is a healthy, happy, productive, successful, fulfilled and blessed life. That's not too much to ask, right?

We must face the truth Life is Hard. Every human being has a Life is Hard moment at some point. As we respond in humility and grace to our hardest moments, our good God anchors us and burnishes off our rough edges. The believer's difference, the believer's impact and the believer's comfort is God. Pressed down and filled up with blessings until we cannot hold anymore. We have the additional everlasting comfort that Heaven is Sure. We will see our loved ones again. Suffering is not the finish. Restoration, bliss and redemption are the last pages of our story. God's goal is different for us because God is Good and because Heaven is sure. This life's happiness is not God's end game. God's goal is that we trust Him in any and all circumstances. As we learn to trust in any and all circumstances, we grow. We are transformed. This is where sanctification begins. This is the gateway to the inside out, upside down kingdom that drew thousands to Christ's side during His public ministry. Drawn to Him, His world and His ways, like others journeying before, we walk miles of dusty Palestine roads traveling endless days with our Messiah. We too, can live out a Faith Worth Having. We too, can be our best when life is at its worst.

Armed with this faith, we labor and pray experiencing God's forever kingdom here and now. We do not need to wait for Heaven to experience God is Good. Yes, life is peppered and at times pummeled with hard moments. Our difficulties are like hidden minefields. We tread carefully trying to avoid the click of a trigger. WHAM! A life altering explosion. Shattered bits and tiny pieces are all that remain from our once seemingly idyllic life. At times, we will feel we are drowning in sorrow. We will never escape the truth Life is Hard. But, we love and serve a good God. We can experience, taste, see, touch, hear and feel God is Good even in the worst of times.

Finally, Heaven is Sure. The ultimate freedom song trusting with everything on the line, we enter into His gates with singing knowing our story doesn't end here on planet earth. Our song plays on and on and on. Evergreen forever is our tomorrow. Light can only shine in the darkness. Turn on a flash light in broad daylight and that narrow beam is invisible. In the dead of night, a small flashlight becomes a huge source of direction as the beam crisply cuts through the darkness. God is Good and Heaven is Sure are truly visible during and after our Life is Hard moments. During those moments, we want to desperately change this unchangeable equation. When in pain, we demand a different way to grow and to mature and in our confusion we ask for things to make sense. We implore God to answer us, to make sense of it all and to bring clarity to the muddy mess that now engulfs us. We plead for God to bring light as we battle the darkness. Remember, God did not intend for our life to be this way. His plan was and is perfection. He went to great lengths to fix the brokenness that surrounds us. One day His forever victory will be revealed, but until that day we have important choices to make.

Why do so few of us reach that place of complete trust putting everything on the line? During a sermon series, our pastor challenged us to accept this immutable truth, that we have a great, invincible, incredible, marvelously surprising He-knows- my-name, Almighty God and the wonderful, powerful, gentle, remarkable, forever-standing in-our-place Jesus. We sat comforted by this mind-blowing truth, then came his warning. When we offer all of ourselves to our God, we need to be ready. He will receive everything we offer. When we consider who God is, isn't our all the very least we should be giving? Many of us balk and shy away from this challenge. When we contemplate giving God our all, we offer only a part of our lives and promise we'll give the rest later. We struggle letting go of who or what we love. We grab tight those we love the most, our family and dear friends. These dear ones are off-limits. Can't we surrender just part way? Can't we put up a boundary, a restriction or leave a limit? "God," we say tenderly, "Don't go in this area. You know how much I love them. I promise you God that I can and will take care of them." In other words, we are telling the God of the universe these people are off limits. We worry and stew. We question can I trust this wild, magnificent, great, gently fierce God with the loves that I would die for? If we could stop long enough to process this thought we would realize God already gave His One and only for us. Of course, we can trust Him with our precious ones! After we have walked sheltered in His mysterious grace, our grip loosens on those we cherish. After we have seen with our own eyes His power and His forever love for our dear ones, our fingers relax and our palms turn upward. Letting go of our greatest loves is not complete surrender, not yet.

After we deal with our deepest reluctance, our withholding loved ones from God's control, the final barrier comes to the surface. It is our hidden shame and darkest fears. Can we bring all of our brokenness, our shame, our guilt, our never measuring up, our complete and utter failures to this glory filled, omnipresent God? Vulnerability begins when there are no masks, no excuses, no "God please do not look deep into my soul where my cavernous sorrows and regrets fester. Please God, I feel completely humiliated. Please look the other way." If we are the offering, then God takes all of us. He even wants our messiness, our worst failures, the failures that were completely our fault. Only when our out of order, busted, wrecked, smashed, defeated selves lay open on the altar, can we truly begin our transformation. God wants all of us. He wants our dear ones and our brokenness. He wants the parts of our story that we attempt to hide. When our brokenness rests in His hands, it becomes beautiful. He wants our utter failures. Morning always follows the night. Dawn always breaks. Darkness always gives way. We struggle to believe anything good can come from our mistakes and our failures, yet the truth God is Good is the balm that heals our deepest wounds.

Most of us would choose growth through discipline over growth through pain. We'd choose a twenty minute session in a state of the art gym two to three times a week over standing up to our shoulders, brutally pounded by frigid ocean waves, gasping for every breath, barely able to hold on. Do we have a choice between growth through discipline and growth through pain? The path we'd like to choose is training and working at our faith. Growth through pain, heart aches, dark streets, disorientation is the path we want to avoid at all costs. If we work hard at the discipline training path and follow all of the rules, can we avoid, skip or move beyond the path of pain? Is there some way to protect ourselves from the thorn ridden, foggy, disorienting, anxiety riddled path of pain? The truth is these two paths are so intertwined they are really one road. A two lane road called "The Day by Day Transformational Trust or Crack Growth Highway." We need both. Both push us. Both help us stay tethered to God and tethered to others. The path of pain lasts for a season. This season can last days, months, years, and unfortunately, even decades. This path of pain is biblical. Many children, men, and women of true faith have struggled with pain. Their "as soon as" moment came right after they obeyed by taking their God driven risk. Pain arrives as jail time, famine, lack of water, shipwreck, bankruptcy, a scary diagnosis, a life altering phone call, deep to the bone and kicked in the gut pain. Life will never ever be the same pain.

We have learned that life will crash into us. We have learned God is not looking for what we often bring to Him our shiny recyclables, our business, our successes or our white sand. He is not looking for the outwardly clean rule-following. He is not looking for the good things we worship alongside of Him or unfortunately above Him. God is looking forward. He desires we each move from mature to complete. God is hoping for absolute trust no matter the circumstances. God desires we live like heroic champions standing on our knees living out A Faith Worth Having. As believers we begin our journey with an encounter with the Holy one, the magnificent one, the one and only one Jesus, but somewhere along the line our sense of self can sneak in. We can set ourselves up as His holy earth-to-heaven helper, His equal partner. We joined the family plan: Father, Son, Holy Spirit and me. There is a big difference between worshipping with a friend or a partner and worshipping the superbly wonderful, indescribable, omnipotent, grace-filled, awe inspiring, personal, magnificent, never failing, ever-loving God.

Other times we can feel we need to earn His love or at the very least we need to "help" Him love. We can honestly wonder why this great God would choose to love us. We can live out our faith with this gnawing feeling God couldn't love us for just us. God must have some reason He loves us. He could only love use because we do something. God loves us for some reason. Because we follow His rules, because we serve Him, because we give above and beyond to Him, because we only hang out with people who love Him, each "because" seeps into everything we think about God and everything we do for Him. We believe He loves because we do something, love someone, give some amount or follow some rule. When trying to understand His love our after-the-fall inadequacies plague our hearts. If only we could see all and know everything, we'd understand what He was doing and we'd be able help Him. It is so subtle, but it is our Genesis 3 moment. Genesis 3:4-6 "tempted by the serpent the women was enticed by the concept she'd know everything" She'd know why. For every crossroad, every question and every concern she would know why. Armed with her tree-of-knowledge-know-how she could help God. She could fix everything and everyone. We believe with all our heart we do know what is best our dear ones, our big and little ones and our dearest loved ones. We know we could fix any problem armed with the right information. Often our prayers are more about helping and fixing then about surrendering or trusting. We can be too casual with our amazingly magnificent God. We can refuse to believe in His everlasting grace-filled love. Frozen by self-focus we live only to please ourselves.

Heaven is Sure. For those who have surrendered their life to God's one and only son Jesus, death is defeated, overcome, conquered and no longer our final state. Defeating death would have been enough, but our looking for ways to bless-us-more God made sure we knew that in His inside out, upside down kingdom the slightest action here on earth will have an impact now and an impact forever in eternity. Because Heaven is Sure, everything we do here and now matters for the future. The smallest gesture matters, because we serve a cosmic, always close, eternal, wildly creative God. And don't forget this is the God who creates overflowing out of barely there. Who creates plenty from a meager offering clutched in little hands? Who multiplies a gift given from the lowest of the low? Who transforms an offering given by the the unseen-a child? Matthew, Mark, Luke and John all record when given two sardines and five rolls what does our water-into-wine maker do? He feeds over 5,000 people from a Palestine lunchable!

If we stop short living only by Life is Hard and God is Good, then we will rally the troops with a sign affixed to our wagon that reads *Holy Huddles R Us*. We will circle up. We will do whatever it takes to retreat, to withdraw, to protect our little ones, our dearest ones and our forever loved ones. How does an "eternity now" focus affect His kingdom here on planet earth? We must keep eternity at the forefront of our thinking to make an impact in this game called life. Eternity has to become part of our everyday so that we will happily give out all we have. We will hurry to give away our sardines and rolls. Death is defeated and your actions matter because Heaven is Sure. Jesus was clear the smallest act matters. A cup of water given in His name matters, a prayer shawl knitted with the strands of compassion matters, a gentle word matters, a cup of coffee shared with a hurting friend matters, a prayer whispered matters, the five dollars we gave to someone in need matters. Even the smallest act can be a forever act and every one matters.

His presence is the breath of heaven to us now. In His presence an authentic worship experience washes over us and floods our souls. We feel an emotional response as tears flow or a jubilant response as our feet skip and our hands jump. We celebrate unable to contain our excitement. We stand in a hushed silence celebrating this is our God. Our finger print designer is near. Our ever-present personal God is spending intimate time with us. This amazingly powerful, wildly mysterious God not only loves us, but He likes us too. His joy is to spend time with us, break bread with us, laugh with us and even tenderly weep with us. (Psalm 16:5-6) "My choice is you, God, first and only. And now I find I'm your choice! You set me up with a house and yard. And then you made me your heir!" He seeks us. He chooses us. He loves you and He loves me. Moving toward God, we breathe in trust and life-giving-oxygen. Moving away from self sufficiency, we exhale self-centeredness. Our burgeoning maturity blossoms as we grow toward becoming complete by completely trusting. The only way to grow is enduring life shattering events while standing on our knees trusting God is good. When we endure the daily agony of walking on bits of broken glass, when we move one foot in front of another, when we power through each monotonous step, we are walking in authentic, deep, resilient trust.

Fixing things, fixing people and fixing problems, when we are "fixing" we circumvent the process that moves us toward God. Those of us drowning in busyness, in over-activity and our white sand, are numbing ourselves so that we are never able to find the time or the energy to reach toward God. Those of us, who turn inward caring only about our own life, complaining about everything we see, thwart our own development. With fixing, numbing or complaining, we short circuit our own growth. Sadly, we never make the kingdom impact we were designed to make. We sit munching on our own sardines and rolls while thousands go hungry. Willing to walk closely with our suddenly-spring-God choosing to trust Him during past heart aches and choosing to trust Him now in the midst of new pain, we walk out of our valley of intense darkness a stronger more empathetic Christ follower completely tender to the core. We can triumphant in our weakness. We know the thorn in our side may never go away. The limp, thoroughly reminding us of our past battles, still remains. Ready for the next battle we limp victoriously, dancing through tears, drawn to the sadness in others and freely giving out our last ounce of comfort. The limp that that made us feel less-than now drives us to His presence where aching eases and joy replenishes.

Whether we have been working at our faith excited to step into the unknown holding on to our everyday, everlasting, by-our-side-always God or whether we are just starting out unsure of what to do to move into what God is doing, live a life that moves toward A Faith Worth Having. No matter where we are may our journey acknowledge Life is Hard. Shout God is Good. Roar Heaven is Sure.

Slow down and refuel. Refuse anything less than a responsive heart. Risk it all and feel God's amazing love. Experience His out-of-thin air answers. Day by Day growth readies our heart to respond. Moving closer and closer to God we have the backbone, the strength and the foundation to move performance off the table and live palms up. We live ready for whatever may come. Now, in hope, in belief, in conviction and in reliance on our One and Only, we are ready to be at our best when life is at its worst. We are ready to stand on our knees simply, utterly and completely trusting Him. Fearless trust dwells inside a responsive heart. As we free fall helpless, nothing to grab, picking up speed, soaring faster and faster, anxiety begins to make inroads, then our firm foundation, our genuinely gentle God simply catches us. Firmly tender, sweetly we fall into His arms. We land safe and sound. Our feet out of harm's way now safely touch the ground. Leaving His mission to His everyday masterpieces, Jesus champions us. We soar making an impact throughout His inside out, upside down kingdom.

Who will we follow? Who will we listen to? Will we trust God is Good when we're in impossible circumstances? As an active part of our trusting God, will we cry out? Will we grasp, stretch, reach out toward the One and Only? We must be in daily conversations with God if we are to engage in His life giving strength. Anger, heartache, raw emotions can be part of this exchange. Remember, we must acknowledge hardships are a part of every story and during our most difficult journeys it is okay to hurt deeply, to cry loudly, to sob uncontrollably and collapse in a heap. We must lovingly accept a mature believer's freak out. Can we lift up encouragements and affirm hope in the chaos? Can we acknowledge the deep sorrow that accompanies these devastatingly hard moments? Dazed and confused, can we reach for words holding fast to God, even if we only hear silence? It is right to simply weep with those whose hearts are broken by the cruelest circumstances. Our faith can stand up to the darkest devastation this dying world hurls our way. Whether standing knee deep in grief, wading through unspeakable sorrow or diving into life's splendor, playfully splashing with ridiculous rejoicing and joyful bliss, we confidently hold on for dear life to A Faith Worth Having!

What is keeping you from A Faith Worth Having? Do you feel spread too thin? Do you feel unfocused? Do you live by the code "my performance is my golden ticket"? Do your ears ring with the constant alarms? If you only hear the tyranny of rules, rituals and white sand maintenance, then you are missing the essential ingredient. You lack knowing and understanding God's greatest desire. What does the everlasting King of Kings want? You, He desires you. You are critical to revealing God to a broken and lost world. Whether you are considered the lowest-of-low, an unseen or a highly visible, seemly important, the center-of-attention, spot-light type, whether important or invisible, you matter and your efforts matter. You know the worthlessness and frailty of worshiping your ego soaked performances. Live palms up and know your efforts on planet earth matter because of one thing. What you do matters because a good God is working through you and has the everlasting future in mind.

Every day before their one meal a group of orphaned boys would hear a devotional. One day in a chapel in Africa instead of a devotion the caregiver told the boys she was going to pick someone to share a thankful prayer. The boy's eyes darted to the ground. Because of the extremely hard circumstances, they were praying survival prayers not thankful prayers. A boy by the name of Jackson was called on. He could not think of what he was thankful for instead he sang a praise song. The next day, a second boy was called on to share his thankful prayer. He stood and began to sing a praise song. Jackson stood and joined him. On the fourth day, there were four boys standing and singing a praise song. By the twelfth day, there were twelve boys singing a praise song. An American dignitary happened to be at the orphanage and heard the boys sing. She said "You need to form a choir and come to the United Sates." She did all the necessary paperwork, and a trip was planned. It was on that trip to America that Jackson met his new family. Because one orphan boy dared to worship his God in the midst of nothing, every orphan boy in that choir found a forever home in the U.S. When I last heard forty five other boys from that orphanage in Africa have been adopted.

I could tell you story after story about how one person has made an enormous difference. These were not VIPs. These were not spot light people. These were often folks who had very little power or money to accomplish small things let alone the great big asks. Forget about make-a-difference dreams. No, these revolutionaries were ordinary folk who simply caught fire and could not look away. With mundane faithfulness, they yielded. They just did that small thing God called them to do. Then, all of the sudden their life touches another and another and another. Darkness is chased away by the tiny flicker of one single candle. In our florescent flooded artificially lit lives, we forget this life altering truth. We forget we have the power to chase away the darkness, even if it is only by one small candle, one tiny flickering flame. Darkness still abounds ever since that fateful day Eve picked and Adam ate. We have all experienced the bottomless shadow. We can choose to trust or choose to crack. We can live Standing on Our Knees with A Faith Worth Having. We can avoid the white sand pitfalls. We can avoid those things that get in our way causing us to spin our wheels and stay stuck munching on our own sardines and rolls.

Life is hard. God is Good. Heaven is Sure. These three strands of thread are not easily broken. They represent three sides of our journey. We must have all three to have a vibrant faith. They are glued together and fused into one by our crucial life-giving endowment called trust. These three truths create a firm foundation for us to understand a confusing world, navigate a complex world and live triumphantly over a broken world. Out in the ether some preach "the name it, claim it, genie on a golden throne, just ask Him and He'll do it for you" kind of faith. Demanding is not faith. There is deep beauty in our awe-inspiring faith. Strong and wonderfully perfect does not begin to describe our transcendent convictions, but there is another part to our journey. It is not the "ignore the trouble, slap a smile on it, pretend everything is okay" kind of faith. Our faith withstands the ripples of aches, the groundswell of anguish, the waves of sorrow, the torrents of injustice and the floods of brokenness. If we broadcast **only** God is Good, we create a false reality. Jesus would never have needed to come. We would be without the depths, the lengths and the breath that our good God provides throughout our mystifying journey of pain. Understanding these truths Life is Hard, God is Good and Heaven is Sure translates into God can be trusted even in the worst of times. These three truths enable us to become fearless champions living brave, not safe, in the inside out, upside down kingdom of God. If we understand these truths Life is Hard and God is Good and through all the hard things God is with us, for us, and does have a plan ending with Heaven is Sure, then and only then, can we begin the transformation into a Christ follower Standing on Our Knees living out A Faith Worth Having.

Delight in these words for your soul

Life is hard. God is Good. Heaven is Sure. Let go. Let it all go. Give it all away. Give away all the control, all the plans, all the safety and all the boundaries that bring a false sense of security. Be brave. May our God, a firm foundation, help us navigate our full-size heart breaks and our irritatingly-little aches. Triumphantly, press toward His forever love. Know each tear shed is recorded in His book. Soar beyond this unpredictable, crazy, overwhelming world. Beautifully strong, wonderfully perfect, faithful to the end, our Savior battles the waves of sorrow, the torrents of injustice and the seas of brokenness. Rush toward the maker of the universe, the victor over the unrelenting darkness, our travel companion during our mystifying journey of pain. He champions us as we battle grief and sorrow within this inside out, upside down kingdom. Fearlessly trust Him. "What can mere mortals do?" Live without any regrets, bathed in love, open to everlasting peace. Gloriously reach beyond our feeble strength. We run determined steps. We run with a forever wind at our back. We run after the God driven risk-takers who have fearlessly gone before. Walk joyously and resiliently. Rest in His shadow and in the warmth of the One and Only. We honor and marvel at every cloud, a flag gloriously marking His faithfulness, His tenderness and His nearness. We are loved by the greatest love. We curl up and cuddle up with the everlasting Papa holding us in His arms forever.

Amen

CHAPTER **13**

Final thoughts

Big J stood between his best buddy Rowan and his other pal Declan. Any other time he would have been laughing it up and messing with his friends being a typical three year old boy, but now he stood there looking extremely uncomfortable. It was our year end celebration. Over the last four months, we had practiced several songs to sing for our family members and loved ones who could grab forty-five minutes to have pizza, ice cream and a piece of cookie cake. The boys were lined up against the wall, and the girls were sitting in little chairs in front. As we began to sing, the faces ranged from zany, crazy happy to extremely uncomfortable. The twin girls sitting next to each other were grabbing the other's face singing as if the rest of the world simply melted away. I had taken Jensen's Minnie mouse ballet slippers away because during our practice when Jensen joyously kicked her feet her right shoe flew off. The first time was funny. The fourth was dangerous. We began singing "If you are happy and you know it" that was when I first saw Big J's face. He did not look happy. He is one of my shy friends. He never spoke when we shared about our weekends. He didn't stand up when I called his name for the Name Game. Even during Show and Tell, the only way I could get him to participate was to have him stay seated secure on the letter rug demonstrating how his toy worked. For him, getting up and walking around a circle of nineteen other three year olds was too much even when armed with his favorite toy from home. Just five feet away from big J, who was now frozen against the wall, stood a hedge of Grandmas, Gigis, Mamas, Papas, Moms, Dads and Aunts. Most of their faces were blocked by their phones. We were on display. Every move was being captured for posterity. As I watched this sweet, shy boy in the midst of the anarchy of singing preschoolers, I was so proud of him. He was hanging tough, uncomfortable as he was, he quietly stood firm. Then, I began to think about his mom and his dad. What did they feel? They were both present. Did they want to rescue him? Did they ache for him? He looked as if he were in physical pain being on display. Did they feel intensely proud that their shy, sweet boy was sticking it out? Showing true grit and strength standing in his weakness, as rough as it was, he stayed put through all four songs in front of all that family paparazzi. One extremely proud teacher raced to his side. She hugged him, then told him what a great job he did. She kissed him on top of his head as he ran to the warmth and safety of his loving parents. Scooping him up in their arms, all three were huddled together now beaming with smiles.

I was excited to now have Auggie in my class. I had enjoyed having his older brother when he was three. He and I became pals. He was a little guy even for three. When we used our hallway bathrooms, Auggie was so little I had to hold him up to the counter, so he could wash his hands. We quickly remedied this with extra step stools. Proudly, he stood washing his own hands. Oh, how three year olds love independence! His family was giving him a nightly shot to increase his growth. They called it his Incredibles shot so that he could become strong and fast. I suppose elasticity or invisibility would have just been a bonus. He was just one of those kids with gorgeous red hair, a gravelly voice, impish smile, eyes that twinkled and a crazy sense of humor. Auggie loved the computer. Passionate and strong Auggie knew his own mind. He let everyone else know exactly what and how he was feeling. During our morning chat while she dropped Auggie off, his Mom and I agreed he could get too attached to his screen time. His allotted five minutes could easily linger into ten. A teacher I worked with for a month didn't believe a child should **ever** be unhappy. That morning when I informed Auggie his time was up on the computer, Auggie was deeply and visibly unhappy. I tried to redirect Auggie. I encouraged him to play with his friends. He began to cry. Then, I watched the other teacher get on her knees holding him in her arms, she begin to cry with him. Her heart may have been in the right place, but all the attention was actually going only prolong Auggie's heart ache. I had to be the bad guy standing there with a firm tone telling him to go play trains or go play cars. I won't even describe the look my co-worker gave me in disgust as she got up. Auggie stood silent for a few minutes. Finally, he found comfort with two friends at our train table. A few moments later he was laughing as only Auggie could.

I had been through several grave site services, so I knew what to expect. It was still hard. It was still that final good bye. What I hadn't expected was to be handed a folded American flag. My brother had made the arrangements for the actual burial. Since my dad was a veteran, we had his casket draped in the flag. I hadn't expected to receive the flag neatly folded during the graveside service. As this man I had never met knelt next to me, he handed me the triangle folded flag. He said, "On behalf of the President of the United States, the Navy and a grateful nation, please accept this flag as a symbol of our appreciation for your loved one's honorable and faithful service." I foolishly thought I had finished crying for the day. I felt my eyes well up with more hot tears. I held the flag close and felt completely overwhelmed, but what is also seared in my memory is her face. A close friend was sitting next to me. I could see from behind her sunglasses the tears were flowing down her cheeks. In my deep grief, I was not alone. I felt loved.

Sometimes God is just a few feet away intensely proud as we stand uncomfortably tall in our weakness. Sometimes He is firm in His redirection as He closes the door and seemly bolts all the nearest windows. We feel He has stepped on our broken heart as He changes our direction or the direction of those we love. Sometimes He is as close as our dearest friend. It can seem as we grieve our tears become His tears. He weeps with us. The concept that God is with us means He is with us in every different kind of outcome. He is nearer than our own breath. He is especially near during difficult challenges as we navigate our Life is Hard moments. He is faithful. He is strong. Never doubt Him. He is near.

Cry out from the bottom of our core and trust God. Avoid the white sand demanding; avoid all the good stuff that can rob us of our eternal impact. Move toward God. We are always moving so move toward God. Day by Day grow. Know small growth leads to a responsive heart ready to handle anything. When life crashes into us, whether it is seemly just a fender bender a heavy lift of a small burden or it is a full head-on collision sending pieces of our lives flying every which way, know both can lead to beautiful, compassionate growth. Tread lightly with each other as we are all a transformed, redeemed, rescue story. Know that there is no earthly pain that Heaven cannot heal. (Psalm 23:4 my version) "Even when we walk exhausted, confused, lost, worried, stretched, hurting, broken through the valley of the shadow of death and dying, the ultimate heart aches, He is beside each one of us. Reach out He is near."

We each have a story to write, a journey to take and a promise to fulfill. We are not in control of the span of our years. We are not in control of the circumstances we face. We are not in control of those we journey with those closest to us and those who have power over us. What we do have power over is our attitudes, our actions and our responses. (John chapter 21:21-22) Referring to the disciple John, Peter asked Jesus this question. "Turning his head, Peter noticed the disciple Jesus loved following right behind. When Peter noticed him, he asked Jesus, 'Master, what's going to happen to *him*?' Jesus said, 'If I want him to live until I come again, what's that to you? You— follow me.'" Each journey is laid out by an all powerful, loving, amazing God. We are prepared by that God to follow Jesus. Walk your own journey. Follow Jesus to A Faith Worth Having.

Remember the woman of faith from the first chapter? I would love to share her triumphant, happily ever after story. What a joy to report God worked in her husband who turned his life over to Jesus becoming a successful, strong, committed believer. I would love to write that all of their material property was redeemed. God blessed them above and beyond with a new home, a better home than the one they lost. They lived out the rest of their days in the warmth of family and friends having just celebrated their sixity-second wedding anniversary. We would cheer and celebrate saying see a life lived well is rewarded here on earth. This is what we desire after tremendous sorrow, right? Redemption must follow suffering. I am intimately familiar with this woman of faith and her impossible journey. Unfortunately, after losing most of her material processions and living in almost impossible circumstances constantly battered by deep financial stress, she received devastating news. Cancer. Not once but twice giving her only eighteen months to live. This, the cruelest portion of her journey, was filled with pain, side effects, vomiting, unrelenting fatigue, more vomiting and a broken body wasting away before our very eyes. What is mind-blowing to me is that I can report her faith never faltered. She battled bravely. She was human. She wept often in the midst of almost unendurable circumstances. After three years without a job, my Dad had finally found employment with benefits. We cheer for God's goodness. Working for only five months, while mom was in the hospital receiving her first chemo treatment, my dad lost that job. We lost all his benefits. Why? Life is Hard.

Again, where was her glorious God? Why harder circumstances not helpful answers? Standing on her knees her faith never faltered. She believed God would heal her. Her faith stood the ultimate test. She finished well. She is the bravest, strongest, most amazing woman I have ever met. Faith, genuine faith, is seen, felt and exercised in the midst of these hardest moments. Faith is also seen in the midst of our celebrations in those magnificent, almost indescribable happy moments. Joy is simply trusting God completely by resting in His opulent, ever present, never late, marvelous love. His love is lived out in all our moments. He is present in all the breath-taking, splendid, skip a beat, warm your soul moments. He is there in the weeping, can't seem to breathe, soul crushing, life altering, unspeakable, terrible moments. Her faith and His love were lived out seemly effortlessly intertwined day after day, hour after hour and minute after difficult minute. Her human frailty seemed to be woven with glorious celestial threads shimmering through each deep, dark, lonely moment she walked. Glory whispered behind her, "I am near. Do not fear. I am here."

It was eleven o'clock at night. The phone rang. It's never good news at eleven o'clock at night. The voice said "Her blood pressure is dropping." My father raced to get dressed hurrying to be at the hospital. He hadn't spent a lot of time with her during her illness. In this moment, he raced to be by her side. I couldn't move. I watched him fly out the door. He offered to take me. Almost unable to speak I uttered, "No thank you." The overwhelming silence and deep titanic sadness fell like a thick fog engulfing the room. I dropped to my knees. It was all I could do. Breathing felt difficult. I don't think anything I said made much sense. My heart inside my chest was beating so hard as I pleaded for God's peace, His presence and His answer. She was being healed as I begged weeping for His redemption. What would overwhelm me and almost crush my soul was her healing took place on the other side. Jesus came. She was ushered into glory. She saw His loving face. Her faith was rewarded beyond what any eye has ever seen. Walking out from the prison called cancer, she awoke whole and perfect in His presence. I am confident cradled in her Savior's arms she heard, "Well done my good and faithful servant. Welcome home"

I was twenty-four when my mom went home to be with her One and Only. A broken heart does not begin to describe my journey for the next twenty years. Unwinding false beliefs, dismantling unwarranted shame and guilt took a toll on this lost, scared, deeply broken, lonely kid. My saving grace, I have held tight to her faith-A Faith Worth Having. I can return to that small apartment on the eastside and feel the carpeting under my knees. I see her daughter all alone broken, helpless, kneeling, crying out, moaning and weeping in despair. I hear myself pleading with God to somehow make sense of this unfathomable loss. Because we were not only mother and daughter, we were the best of friends. We had a deep bond. We had walked a broken path together. We had endured grief together. We had cried together. We played, loved and laughed together. She was my true north, my mentor and my pal. She was amazing. She was my wonderfully funny, other focused, sweetly gracious, ferociously loyal mom. But now when I look back at that scene, I see something new. I am kneeling, weeping and pleading, but I am not alone. Kneeling next to me is the One and Only. I see Jesus holding onto me as I attempt to hold onto Him. His arms cover me as I wait to hear the final news, "She is gone. She is home at last." She was out of pain and never again going to experience loss. She was safe. She was home. I see Him hold me, comfort me, words cannot describe the feeling of losing my special someone while being held by my Everything.

Walking through the shadow of death brings clarity and depth to our everyday lives. I look back now and I see a daughter standing on her knees while her beloved mother leaves this world now standing seeing her Savior face to face. Home at last. Well done my good and faithful servant. Well done. The Father has prepared things no eye has seen. Welcome home!

Life is Hard. God is Good. And Heaven is Sure. May these words launch you into the inside out, upside down kingdom living out your Faith Worth Having making your forever impact changing this world for the better.

Make a run for God you won't regret it.

Live out an authentic walk with the mystery maker, great forgiver, the ferocious lover. Celebrate with dancing hands, raised hearts, joyful tears and exuberant singing. Experience God's more-than-enough drenched in His everlasting satisfaction each life surrounded by suddenly spring moments. May your every day overflow with arm-loads-of-blessings. May grace graffiti be painted on the walls, fences and tunnels of your life. Secure in His presence release every earth bound thought. Bank His promises in the vault of your heart. Stand in Awe of God's yes comforted by His help. Surprised by His protection when we thought we knew better, but now we see his life-saving "no," realizing the wisdom of His "not now," the good judgment of His "wait a few years" and the protection of His "take a different road." Have a God shaped life. Live in His all-generous love, His holy splendor, His always there, in our past, in our present and in our future. He is always close never far. We are His invited guests to a forever celebration a forever life glorious, a life garlanded with grace and a life festooned with beauty. We are welcomed directly by Him. He calls us by our name. His unmistakable voice, that gentle voice speaks our name as only He can. We hear our name sheltered in His love. We turn. We run toward Him. With no regrets, we run completely transformed decked out in His delight, sheathed in His glory and wrapped in His splendor. To audibly hear our name from His lips, I can't imagine a more glorious moment. A divine conspiracy. A suddenly spring moment. When at last. We see Him face to face. We hear, "Welcome home my love. I have been waiting for so long to see you. Welcome home, my faithful one, welcome home."

Life is hard
God is Good
Thank you God,
Thank God
Heaven is Sure.

Amen

About the Author

Susan Rosecrans has lived in Indiana her entire life. She has been a preschool teacher for twenty years. She stumbled into writing after sharing thoughts about faith with the Drama Team at Grace Church in Noblesville, IN. Having walked almost her entire life as a believer, she became fascinated with the idea of a faith worth having. Who doesn't want a gritty, remarkable, astounding, quiet, daring, leaping-into-the-unknown kind of faith? What does that kind of faith look like? She began her journey to learn about that kind of faith. This book is her story searching for A Faith Worth Having.